DREAMWEAVER

The Bohemian Entrepreneur's Odyssey
of Turning Dreams into Reality.

I0347910

Innovative Leadership: Inspiring Modern
Business with Creativity and Positive Energy

MARKUS HOFER

Dreamweaver

Copyright © Markus Hofer 2024

The Author has asserted their rights under the Copyright Act 1968 (the Act) to be identified as the author of this work.

All rights reserved. No part of this publication may be reproduced, stored in a retrieval system, or transmitted in any form or by any means, electronic, mechanical, photocopying, recording or otherwise, without the prior written permission of the author. Any person who does any unauthorised act in relation to this publication may be liable to criminal prosecution and civil claims for damages.

The Australian Copyright Act 1968 (the Act) allows a maximum of one chapter or ten per cent of this book, whichever is the greater, to be photocopied for educational purposes by an educational institution holding a statutory education licence provided that the educational institution (or body that administers it) has given a remuneration notice to the Copyright Agency (Australia) under the Act.

ISBN: 978-1-923163-65-2
       978-1-923512-37-5

Self-Published by Markus Hofer with assistance by Clark & Mackay

Proudly printed in Australian by Clark & Mackay

INTRODUCTION

The Extraordinary Journey of Markus Hofer – A Life in Business and Beyond

In the tapestry of life, Markus Hofer's journey is a remarkable blend of passion, resilience, and the pursuit of dreams. Born in Munich to Austrian parents, Markus's life unfolded against the stunning backdrop of snow-capped alps, sparking a lifelong love affair with skiing. His journey, however, traverses continents and industries, weaving together a narrative of business ventures, cultural exploration, and the relentless pursuit of his aspirations.

After pursuing his love for skiing and working as a ski instructor in Austria, Markus's journey took an unexpected turn to the sunburnt landscapes of Australia. There, in the picturesque Perisher Valley, he honed his skills, spending half the year in the Southern Hemisphere and the other half back in the heart of Europe.

Markus's life took an exciting turn as he delved into hotel management studies, sowing the seeds for his entrepreneurial spirit. This passion led to the creation of a five-star hotel in Tirol, evolving into a sprawling 300-bed wellness resort – a testament to his vision and determination. A bold move to Australia saw Markus becoming a McDonald's franchisee, opening stores in Maroubra and Coogee Beach, contributing to the fast-food landscape of Sydney.

A serendipitous encounter on a ski trip to Canada introduced Markus to Starbucks Coffee, igniting a pursuit that would result in a partnership to introduce the iconic brand to Australia. Yet, as paths diverged, Markus sold his share to the mother company, paving the way for a new chapter in the sun-soaked haven of Byron Bay.

Markus's Australian adventure continued as he purchased an iconic café in Byron Bay's main street. However, the complexities of the partnership led to the sale of the business, marking the beginning of a truly extraordinary chapter – The Bohemian in Bali. Nestled in the thriving heart of Canggu, this understated boutique hotel became a canvas for artistic and designer aspirations, a testament to Markus's unwavering commitment to authenticity and heart-driven ventures.

The Bohemian in Bali is not just a hotel; it is a culmination of Markus's life experiences, a testament to the lessons learned along the way. This book is a humble summary of those learning's – a journey through the highs and lows of business, the unexpected turns, and the triumphs that come from a heart fully invested in the pursuit of dreams. As we explore Markus's insights, we embark on a journey that transcends business, offering a glimpse into the soul of an entrepreneur who dares to dream and, against all odds, turns those dreams into reality.

CHAPTER 1

A Foreigner in the Country I Was Born In Beyond Borders

In the heart of Munich, a city steeped in history, I began my journey as a foreigner in the land of my birth. Born to Austrian parents who had transplanted themselves from the rugged terrain of Tirol to the bustling streets of Munich, I emerged into a world where the echoes of my heritage resonated against the backdrop of a new life.

My father, a man of resilience, moulded by the hardships of post-war Tirol, came from a family of 13. Driven by an unyielding desire for financial success, he sought a brighter future and married my mother, a daughter of a doctor and an entrepreneurial woman who ran a tobacco shop in Innsbruck. Their union marked the beginning of a journey that would shape the trajectory of my life.

In pursuit of prosperity, my parents moved from the rugged landscapes of Tirol to the vibrant city of Munich. The success my father found in property development elevated our lifestyle, affording us yachts in the Mediterranean and holiday houses that stood as testaments to our newfound privilege. However, the allure of financial success came at a cost, and the strains it placed on my parents' marriage led to a divorce that would dramatically alter the course of my life.

From the penthouse luxury to the austerity of a social housing estate in the less affluent corners of Munich, my world shifted drastically. I found solace in simplicity, adapting to a life without the opulence that once defined us. Our visits to the mountains, to a home with no electricity, no running water, and certainly no television, became the grounding force that connected me to a different reality.

Working on the land in the Austrian Alps became my sanctuary, and the mountains, my refuge. The dichotomy of my life in Munich, where I felt like a guest in my own country, and the gravitational pull of the Austrian peaks, created a tension that permeated my school years. Academic pursuits felt mundane, and the pull from the mountains disrupted any semblance of settling into the routine of school life.

It was clear; I was a wanderer in this city, marking time until the day I could make my home in the mountains of Austria permanently. School became a challenge; the academic results were average, except for mathematics, a subject that came effortlessly to me. The classroom failed to ignite my passion, leaving me perpetually bored with the feeling that I was being told things I already knew.

Sports became my sanctuary, with skiing emerging as the forefront of my pursuits. The annual ski camps were the highlights, and winning the school ski championships every year revealed an early glimpse of success – a realisation that I could excel when immersed in activities I loved. Skiing, it seemed, was destined to be more than a pastime; it was to become the guiding force in my life.

As I eagerly awaited the end of high school, a burning desire to pursue my passion for skiing and to return to Tirol, to the mountains that called me, fuelled my impatience. The confines of the classroom could no longer contain the aspirations of a young man yearning to carve his path in the alpine landscapes that held his heart. Graduation, for me, was not just an academic milestone but the gateway to a life where the mountains would become not just a backdrop but a way of life.

CHAPTER 2

`'Artistry in Rebellion'`

Although the academic portion of my school life was not to my liking, I found great joy and success in the diverse experiences offered by the Steiner education system. As the gates of my Steiner-like school swung open, I entered a realm of education that was more than a curriculum – it was a canvas for creativity, a haven for social consciousness, and a stage for rebellion. Nestled outside Munich, this school became my sanctuary during the tumultuous 70s, an era marked by the rhythmic heartbeat of the hippy movement.

The Tapestry of Rebellion

In the 70s, my school was not just a place of learning; it was a microcosm of rebellion against the status quo. Long hair, bell-bottom jeans and a chorus of like-minded students defined the landscape. The air resonated with the tunes of protest, as we, the children of the flower power generation, lent our voices to causes that stirred our collective conscience.

The Hippy Period's Palette

Against a backdrop of artistic expression and free-spirited exploration, the school embraced the hippy ethos. Here, the conventional boundaries of education dissolved, and in their place emerged an environment steeped in art, music and a spirit of questioning. We weren't just students; we were participants in a grand experiment of social consciousness.

Creativity as the Curriculum

In this alternative educational haven, the curriculum extended beyond textbooks. Art became a language, and creativity was the currency of expression. From painting to poetry, the school fostered an environment where our imaginations were given free rein. It was here that I first dipped my toes into the vast ocean of artistic expression.

Social Activism as a Subject

The classroom wasn't just a space for lectures; it was a crucible for shaping young minds into socially conscious individuals. The left-leaning ideology of the 70s permeated our studies, inspiring us to question capitalism and challenge the established norms. Social activism became a subject in itself, with lessons extending beyond the walls of our classrooms and into the heart of societal change.

Protests and the Power of Unity

As the era raged with protests against nuclear power and the stationing of bombs on German soil, my school emerged as a hotbed of dissent. In unity, we challenged the authority, questioning the decisions that could shape our future. The power of collective action unfolded in the protests that echoed through the corridors and spilled onto the streets.

Environmental Stewardship as a Principle

Amidst the fervour of rebellion, a quieter yet equally profound theme threaded through our education – environmental consciousness. The seed of environmental stewardship was planted, blossoming into a fundamental principle that would later influence my journey as an entrepreneur. The importance of sustainability and harmony with nature became ingrained in our collective ethos.

Shaping a Socialistic Capitalistic Mindset

While the school may not have explicitly labelled itself as such, its teachings laid the groundwork for a socialistic capitalistic mindset. The marriage of social consciousness with a spirit of entrepreneurship germinated in the minds of students like me. The dichotomy of challenging capitalism while harbouring dreams of creating one's path in the world took root.

The Legacy of a Hippy Education

As bell-bottom jeans swayed with the rhythm of the times, and the scent of idealism lingered in the air, my Steiner-like school bestowed upon me more than just academic knowledge. It cultivated an ethos – a philosophy of rebellion, artistic expression, social consciousness and a questioning spirit that would echo through the corridors of my mind for years to come.

The hippy period wasn't just a chapter in history; it was a living canvas upon which the seeds of my entrepreneurial mindset were sown. In the kaleidoscope of the 70s, my school became a masterpiece of rebellion, shaping not just students but future thinkers who would dare to question, dream and eventually redefine the business landscape.

CHAPTER 3

**Lessons in the Shadows –
Escaping the Job from Hell**

My initiation into the workforce unfolded in the heart of Munich, within the sprawling confines of 'Sport Scheck', the city's largest sports emporium. This initial foray into the professional realm would become a crucible of lessons, where the shadows of a negative encounter would leave an indelible mark on my journey.

The Buzz of Sport Scheck

The vibrant energy of Munich's bustling city life mirrored the pulsating heartbeat of 'Sport Scheck.' As a sales assistant in this sporting haven, I eagerly embraced the prospect of working in a domain I cherished. However, my anticipation soon collided with the reality of my first encounter with a manager – an encounter that would shape my understanding of leadership forever.

A Managerial Letdown

My manager, the supposed guiding force of our team, revealed himself to be an embodiment of condescension. Indifferent to the needs of the staff and customers alike, he only graced us with his presence when the scrutinising eyes of top management loomed. A leader in title only, he showcased no interest in fostering a positive work environment. The disconnection between his managerial role and his leadership presence created an unpleasant atmosphere, infecting the very core of the business with what I could only describe as 'bad energy'.

Navigating the Dark Currents

The toxicity emanating from this manager cast a pall over our workspace, creating an atmosphere where motivation waned and camaraderie dwindled. The very essence of what should have been an enjoyable and fulfilling experience soured under the oppressive cloud of negativity. My instinctual response was to distance myself from this unfavourable energy, as I sought solace in the looming shadows of the Austrian Alps – a sanctuary that held the promise of renewal.

The Call of the Mountains

With the power of the mountains beckoning me, I began reaching out to friends in the skiing community, exploring the potential for opportunities back in Austria. The vision of a winter season spent amidst the alpine landscapes offered a beacon of hope in stark contrast to the gloom of my current workplace. A lead soon materialised into a job offer in a small Tyrolean ski resort, just an hour and a half from Munich. Impatiently, I endured the oppressive environment in Munich, eagerly awaiting the escape to the crisp mountain air.

From Hell to Alpine Haven

As winter finally descended, I bid farewell to the soul-draining job in Munich and relocated to a shared room in the cellar of the ski school building. Sharing quarters with six fellow instructors, the camaraderie and the mountainous backdrop felt like a reprieve from the oppressive atmosphere I had left behind. The transformation from the job from hell to the camaraderie of the ski school seemed like a transition from the shadows to the light.

An Indelible Mark

Yet, as I settled into my new alpine haven, the lessons from the job in Munich lingered. The memory of the negative person and the pervasive bad energy he exuded had etched itself into the fabric of my consciousness. It was a stark reminder that leadership was not merely a title but a responsibility – a lesson that would guide me as I navigated the uncharted waters of my future career.

A Shattered Illusion and a Learned Lesson

My first job became a symphony of contrasts – a discordant blend of negativity and indifference that led me to seek refuge in the pristine slopes of the Austrian Alps. The shadows of a disillusioned managerial encounter left me with a profound lesson – an understanding that leadership, to be authentic, must be vested in genuine care, connection and the cultivation of positive energy. Little did I know that this chapter, fraught with challenges, would be the precursor to a journey of self-discovery and a commitment to fostering environments that resonate with the empowering energy of the mountains.

CHAPTER 4

Alpine Dreams – Embracing the Ski Instructor's Journey

In the crisp embrace of early November in Tyrol, a small cadre of newly minted ski instructors gathered on a cold morning, eager to embark on a journey that transcended the freezing temperatures. The excitement hung thick in the mountain air as we donned our instructor uniforms – vintage jackets proudly displaying the emblem of the ski school. The attire may have been second hand, weathered by countless seasons on the slopes, but the emblem bore the weight of tradition, signalling our initiation into the world of ski instruction.

A Symphony of Passion

As we gathered in that frozen dawn, the camaraderie was palpable. Each face radiated with a shared passion for skiing, a love that eclipsed the biting cold and the simplicity of our makeshift uniforms. The air echoed with the hum of anticipation, and I felt a profound sense of belonging – a feeling that, for the first time in my life, I was exactly where I was meant to be.

The Humble Insignia

Our uniforms, though worn and weathered, held a power beyond their material form. They transformed us from a group of individuals into a collective force, united by the singular mission of imparting the joy of skiing to eager beginners. The emblem on our jackets was a humble insignia that bridged the gap between our shared passion and the responsibility we had taken on. It was a symbol of our commitment, a badge of honour that we wore with pride.

Home in the Mountains

The accommodations were humble – a shared room with six fellow instructors. Little money, the daily ritual of scraping ice off my aging VW Beetle and the occasional challenge of getting stuck in the snow – all inconveniences that paled in comparison to the grandeur of the mountains that enveloped us. The room became a haven, a place of respite where stories of the slopes were exchanged and friendships were forged.

Passion Trumps Adversity

Even when rain fell and we were left cold and wet, the joy of teaching people how to ski, the allure of the mountains and the prospect of meeting fascinating individuals from around the globe overshadowed any discomfort. Our days were filled with the spirit of holidays, the thrill of adventure and the pulse of festivities. There was a magic in the air, an enchantment that rendered inconveniences inconsequential.

The Power of the Uniform

Ah, the uniform – an emblem of authority, a magnet for attention and a catalyst for endless nights of revelry. With the ski school emblem stitched on our jackets, we became more than instructors; we were the architects of unforgettable experiences, the conduits of alpine magic. Girls flocked to our group, drawn to the allure of the uniform and the promise of endless nights that blurred into mornings.

A Life Beyond Negativity

Lack of sleep, the financial constraints, the challenges of daily life – all faded into the background as the passion for what we did eclipsed any negativity. Life, in its simplicity, became extraordinary. We had nothing in the material sense, but in the realm of shared passion and collective purpose, we were rich beyond measure.

Skiing Into Bliss:

In the crisp alpine air, amid the towering peaks and the exhilarating slopes, I discovered a life rich in simplicity and abundant in joy. The ski instructor's journey, with its humble beginnings and makeshift uniforms, became a symphony of shared passion, forming the backdrop for unforgettable stories, enduring friendships and the magical alchemy of turning the ordinary into the extraordinary. As we glided down the slopes, we weren't just teaching skiing; we were carving the contours of a life deeply immersed in the beauty of the mountains and the boundless enthusiasm of those who dared to dream in the crisp embrace of the Tyrolean winter.

CHAPTER 5

Lost in Translation – A Ski Instructor's Global Odyssey

The culmination of weeks of rigorous training heralded the dawn of my professional ski instructor journey. The crisp mountain air tingled with anticipation as I stood at the meeting spot for the ski school, surrounded by hundreds of eager beginners, each awaiting the assignment of their instructor. Little did I know that this day would mark the beginning of an unforeseen adventure – one that would teach me more than I ever imagined.

Awaiting Destiny

As the sun painted the snow-covered peaks with hues of gold, my excitement was palpable. The air buzzed with the collective energy of both instructors and students, a symphony of anticipation. My elation would be short-lived, as I heard my name called and was directed towards a group of Australians and New Zealanders.

Lost in Translation:

My heart sank as I realised the gravity of the situation. My claim of proficiency in English on the job application came back to haunt me. It became painfully clear that my understanding of English fell short of the linguistic demands of my newfound students. In that moment, I wished I had paid more attention in English classes, as I grappled with the realisation that fudging details on a CV was a lesson learned the hard way.

Navigating the Language Barrier

With no option to retreat, I faced the challenge head-on. Sign language, coupled with the limited English words I could muster, became my linguistic arsenal. The struggle to communicate morphed into a dance of gestures, expressions and laughter. It was a humbling experience but one that forced me to adapt and improvise in the face of adversity.

The Australians Unveiled

As I stumbled through my first encounters with Australians and New Zealanders, I was met with a revelation. Far from the stereotypes I had conjured, they were a vibrant, worldly, open-minded and fun-loving bunch. My preconceptions crumbled as I discovered a culture that transcended the confines of my imagination. Ski resorts in Australia? It was a revelation that set the stage for a transformative winter.

A Life-Changing Encounter

My misadventure in communication would lead to a life-changing encounter. Teaching Australians throughout the winter unfolded as an unexpected journey of cultural exchange. The slopes became a canvas where language barriers melted away, and the universal language of skiing took centre stage. The bond forged on those alpine slopes transcended words, creating memories and connections that would resonate long after the snow had melted.

Lessons Beyond Language

As I navigated the challenges of language and culture, I discovered that ski instruction was not just about imparting technical skills;

it was a conduit for cultural exchange and mutual understanding. The Australians and New Zealanders became more than students; they became ambassadors of a world beyond my own. In the face of linguistic hurdles, I learned the value of genuine connection and the transformative power of embracing the unknown. The encounter with my Down Under students was not just a winter assignment; it was a journey that would broaden my horizons, challenge my assumptions and enrich my life in ways I had never imagined.

CHAPTER 6

**A Pause in the Mountains
- A Twist of Fate**

As the curtain fell on my first season as a ski instructor, the prospect of a summer job seemed elusive. Seeking adventure, I agreed to participate in a ski photo shoot on a glacier in Germany after the instructing job concluded. This decision would be a fateful twist in my journey.

From Mountains to Munich

Returning to Munich, I eagerly embraced the prospect of the photo shoot. However, adversity struck with an unexpected force. While attempting an aerial jump for the shoot, I suffered a major injury – an unmistakable snap echoed through the mountains as my femur fractured. The dream of a second season as a ski instructor evaporated as I faced a long and arduous road to recovery.

A Halt in the Journey

Several operations were needed to address the severity of my injury, putting skiing, let alone ski instructing, out of the question for the next 12 months. The mountains that had once been my sanctuary now felt distant, and the thrill of gliding down the slopes seemed like a distant memory.

An Intervention and a New Path

During this period of forced hiatus, my mother intervened, urging me to consider an alternative path – studying hotel management. Following my mother's advice, I enrolled in a well-regarded hotel management program at a college in Tegernsee, Germany. This academic pursuit harmonised perfectly with my passion for ski instructing, allowing me to tailor my class schedule around my time on the slopes. The proximity of the college to the ski resort, a mere 30-minute drive, further facilitated this balance, enabling me to weave together my educational and sporting aspirations seamlessly.

The conservative nature of Hotel Fachschule initially clashed with my unconventional spirit, but with my passion for skiing on hold, I begrudgingly persevered, balancing my studies with stints working in my father's restaurant. My father achieved his ambition by launching an upscale Italian restaurant named La Forchetta in a prestigious area of Munich, where I lent a hand in various roles, primarily at the bar and in the kitchen.

Compensation was sporadic, but the invaluable experience I gained in the hospitality sector was the true reward and my main objective. I found solace in the routine, albeit with a yearning for the mountains.

Return to the Alps

As the wheels of my new work life turned, the magnetic pull of the mountains became irresistible. A plan took shape – I would return to Tyrol and work in the ski school ski shop, all while still attending classes at college and working occasionally at my father's restaurant. The allure of being surrounded by friends of shared passion and the snowy peaks proved too enticing to resist.

Winter Beckons

Winter returned, and I found myself back in the snow, albeit without the ability to ski. Sneaking in a few runs here and there, I couldn't completely stifle the craving for the rush of wind against my face as I descended the slopes. The Australians returned, and old friends from the previous year re-joined the alpine landscape.

Dreams of Down Under

Amidst the snow-capped peaks, plans to visit Australia took shape. The idea of instructing skiing in the Southern Hemisphere beckoned, offering a new chapter in my adventurous journey. With the Australians as friends and an unyielding passion for the slopes, the prospect of an Australian winter became an enticing possibility.

A Twist Unravelled

The twist of fate that began with a seemingly routine photo shoot had altered the course of my journey. From a broken femur to a hotel management college, the unexpected turns paved the way for a return to the mountains, albeit in a different capacity.

As winter once again painted the landscape in white, the allure of skiing, albeit restricted, remained steadfast. The next chapter would lead me across oceans to a land Down Under (Australia), where the snow, the slopes and a new adventure awaited.

CHAPTER 7

Down Under Dreams – A Journey to Perisher

With the names and addresses of ski schools in hand, I took a leap of faith and sent out a solitary application – to Perisher, the largest ski resort in Australia. Having recovered from my injuries and armed with additional ski instructor qualifications earned in Austria, along with a freshly minted hotel management diploma, I received a job offer from Alex Heidbauer, an Austrian overseeing Perisher Ski School.

Anticipation and a Long-haul Odyssey

With limited funds but boundless excitement, I embarked on my first long-haul journey –

an epic 48-hour odyssey with five stops from Munich to Sydney. The magnitude of the adventure became apparent as I stepped into a world unlike any I had known.

New Horizons in Sydney

Arriving in Sydney, I found myself in a city that teemed with vibrancy, overwhelming yet captivating. Staying with friends, I soon realised that my savings might not last until the ski season commenced. In a pragmatic move, I secured a job at 'Sport Ski' on George Street. Little did I know that this ski shop would become another home away from home.

Work Life in Australia – A Pleasant Surprise

In the midst of the Sydney hustle, 'Sport Ski' revealed a different work culture – one that was fun, motivating and fundamentally different from what I had experienced in Europe. The owners were not distant figures but eager mentors, offering assistance and coaching. Colleagues were not just co-workers; they were comrades in the shared pursuit of success. It was a novel way of doing business, characterised by leadership, positive energy and a notable absence of threats and discouragement.

Fun, Money, and the Sydney Lifestyle

Work life in Australia was a revelation. It was not just a means to an end; it was an enjoyable and enriching experience. The atmosphere was filled with positivity, motivation and a genuine eagerness to help one another. The financial rewards were good and life – for the first time in a long while – felt easy.

A Love Affair with Sydney

Living in Sydney was a new and fascinating chapter. The beaches, with their golden sands and azure waters, were a revelation of freedom that I had not known before. The city pulsated with life, offering a sense of liberation and adventure that fuelled my newfound love affair with Australia. Forming friendships in Sydney unveiled a new perspective on the city, revealing a lifestyle where work and life balance harmoniously – a stark contrast to the German or Austrian ethos, where it often feels like you live to work, rather than work to live.

A Paradigm Shift

As I settled into work and life in Sydney, the stark differences between the work cultures of Europe and Australia became apparent. The positive energy, supportive leadership and a sense of camaraderie transformed work into a source of joy. Sydney, with its allure and opportunities, marked the beginning of a transformative chapter – one that not only shaped my professional journey but also enriched my life in ways that transcended the boundaries of the professional sphere.

CHAPTER 8

A Snowy Odyssey – Perisher Unveiled

As my time in Sydney swiftly passed, the eagerly awaited day arrived – the commencement of my journey in to Perisher. A friend generously offered a ride from Sydney to Jindabyne, my home for the next four months. The vastness of Australia became apparent during the drive, leaving an indelible impression. The absence of snow along the way was an oddity, and even upon arriving in Jindabyne, the absence of the familiar white landscape was somewhat disappointing.

The Dismal Welcome

My accommodation in Jindabyne left much to be desired – four of us crammed into a hotel room. Yet, the anticipation of snow-covered mountains fuelled my excitement. The actual snow, however, remained elusive. As my starting day approached, the atmosphere was tinged with both eagerness and a sense of remoteness.

The Journey to Perisher

The day finally arrived, and I found myself on the instructor bus from Jindabyne, surrounded by seasoned veterans of the slopes. The drive through the snowy landscape unfolded like a cinematic masterpiece. Around Sponars Creek, the first snow appeared and past Smiggins, over the crest, the entire vista transformed into a breathtaking canvas of white mountains – small and flat but undeniably captivating. The beauty was stark, the air cold and brisk, a stark departure from the almost summer-like Jindabyne.

Induction and Familiar Faces

Summoned to the meeting spot for the ski school, I found myself amidst mostly Austrian colleagues. The familiarity was comforting yet tinged with a sense of strangeness. On that very day, an old colleague from Austria was also beginning his journey in Perisher. Little did I know that this chance encounter would lead to a lasting friendship and professional collaboration, with our paths crossing many more times in the years to come.

Perisher Unveiled

Perisher, with its blanketed slopes, proved to be exciting and inspiring. My boss, Alex, was a beacon of organisation, inspiration and no-nonsense management. The start was slow for all of us, but the season eventually unfolded into one of record snowfalls, financial success and unbridled fun. The long hours of work, the absence of days off and the scarcity of parties were a stark departure from the Austrian ski culture. However, it was a departure we embraced and loved. Perisher became more than a workplace; it became a realm of shared passion, camaraderie and the sheer joy of navigating snow-covered landscapes.

CHAPTER 9

A Life in Winter – Dreams of a Chalet in Austria

From this point onward, life became a perpetual winter, interrupted only by the brief interludes of summer during my trips between Europe and Australia. The absence of internet and mobile phones marked an era where connections were tangible, and phone calls home required meticulous planning. Exotic destinations like Bangkok, Maldives, Hawaii, LA and New York became the backdrop of our summers, each place an eye-opener.

The 80s Adventure

The 1980s were a time of exploration, devoid of the digital connectivity we take for granted today. I roamed the world, soaking in experiences, drawing inspiration, making comparisons and always reconnecting with friends forged on the snowy slopes. Amidst this global exploration, the time spent in Austria lost some of its lustre. The pay was incomparable to Australia, and the ski school's organisation seemed stuck in a bygone era.

Shift in Focus

Comparisons were inevitable, and the allure of working in Austria diminished. The emphasis shifted to family visits and the simple joy of being in familiar surroundings. Australia offered financial rewards beyond what Austria could match, thanks to a favourable exchange rate. Savings became the primary focus, and an opportunity to invest in Austrian land emerged.

Dreams of a Chalet

As I accumulated experiences, ideas germinated. My extensive time with ski holidaymakers in Austria and Australia had given me unparalleled insights into what guests truly desired. Detailed market research unfolded, surpassing what anyone else could have achieved. Plans took shape for a small wine bar with chalet accommodations – a village-style setup blending seamlessly with the surrounding nature, echoing a rustic mountain style.

Land Acquisition

With dreams outlined and plans drawn, the missing piece of the puzzle was the capital. An opportunity to purchase land in Austria emerged, and I seized it. The vision was clear, and the potential for a chalet-style haven resonated with the essence of the region. Nature, authenticity and a touch of *Heidi* were to be woven into every aspect of this envisioned alpine retreat.

In this chapter of our journey, the seeds of a new venture were sown, waiting for the right moment to sprout and transform into the mountain retreat I had envisioned – a haven that would capture the spirit of the Alps and offer a respite for those seeking the charm of a winter wonderland.

CHAPTER 10

**The Three F's – Friends,
Family and Dreams Deferred**

Raising capital for my alpine dream became a journey through the realms of the three F's: friends, family and – though I hoped otherwise – not fools. As fate would have it, family emerged as my main pillar of support, with my father investing in my aspirations. The local bank manager, an ex-ski instructor colleague, also played a crucial role in financing my dream.

Navigating the Complex Terrain

While my savings had been channelled into planning, permits, consulting and licenses, I continued to work in the snowy fields of Australia and back in Austria while construction commenced. The initial signs of stress appeared as I navigated a landscape unfamiliar to a 24-year-old and dealt with architects unaccustomed to working with inexperienced clients.

Dreams Meet Reality

Compromising on design became a recurring theme, and the dreams I had envisioned collided with the harsh reality of a commercial, heartless world. Everything seemed to revolve around cost considerations and the stubbornness of those around me. The idealistic vision clashed with the pragmatic demands of the construction process, leaving me grappling with the stark realisation that dreams, once so vivid, were slipping into the sobering realm of practicality.

The Challenge of Divergent Ideas

The project became a melting pot of conflicting thoughts and ideas. Navigating the diverse opinions proved challenging, with each invested party bringing their own perspectives and demands. The idealistic vision faced the hard truth of compromise, cost considerations and the inherent challenges of bringing together a myriad of perspectives.

As the chapter unfolded, the dream encountered its first set of challenges, revealing the stark contrast between the world of dreams and the unyielding reality of turning those dreams into bricks and mortar. The journey had begun, and the path ahead seemed both daunting and laden with lessons.

CHAPTER 11

The Grand Opening – A Stroke of Luck and Australian Spirit

The momentous day arrived the grand opening of my alpine retreat. A stroke of luck smiled upon me as a substantial number of bookings poured in, largely from my Australian connections forged through years of working with Australians. This stroke of luck laid the foundation for the dream start every aspiring entrepreneur envisions – almost 100 per cent occupancy.

A Team of Dreamers

With the hotel bustling at full capacity, the real work began. Early mornings ushered in the hustle of serving breakfast, followed by shuttling guests to the ski lifts, office work and tending to the bar during dinner service. My youth was an asset, fuelling my drive to make it work. A small but dedicated team, including Sigi, my old ski instructor colleague from Australia now working with me and another ski instructor couple assisting in the restaurant in exchange for lodging and meals, created a dynamic ensemble. We were not just colleagues; we were friends united by a common goal, injecting a sense of fun into our work and extending the same camaraderie to our guests.

A Fusion of Friendships

The feedback was overwhelmingly positive, with many guests rebooking for the following year or venturing to join us during the summer months. Friendships blossomed, blurring the lines between guests and hosts. The warm rapport extended beyond the transactional nature of hospitality, and our guests became integral members of our burgeoning friendship group.

Challenges with German Guests

However, as with any venture, challenges surfaced. Dealing with German guests proved to be a different terrain. My adopted Australian way of life didn't always align seamlessly with the German mentality. Yet, despite the occasional clash of cultures, our commitment to creating a welcoming environment managed to resonate, maintaining a steady stream of income.

The opening chapter of the hotel marked not only a professional milestone but also the crystallisation of friendships and a communal spirit that would come to define the essence of our alpine retreat. The dream was not just materialising; it was flourishing into a vibrant reality woven with the threads of shared joy, hard work and the bonds formed in the snowy embrace of the Austrian Alps.

CHAPTER 12

Navigating Growth – Lessons Learned and Expansion Unveiled

Entering the realm of our dream project with youthful exuberance, I chose to defy professional advice, convinced that energy and passion could overcome any challenge. However, the initial stage of my journey unveiled the first major lessons – lessons borne from ignorance and a lack of heed for sage counsel.

The Bitter Pill of Reality

I found myself inadequately equipped with knowledge, having disregarded the warnings of financial advisors who had cautioned against a business scale too diminutive to yield profits and a return on investment. The echoes of the finance professor's words reverberated: *Masse is Kasse*, a German adage signifying that volume equates to profits. My idyllic mountain retreat, while rich in spirit, proved too modest to generate sufficient income to cover expenses and carve out a profit. Hard work became a futile pursuit in the absence of financial rewards.

Escaping Forward

In response to this revelation, a strategic decision emerged – to escape forward. I devised plans to expand, enhance and augment our offerings. The vision encompassed the incorporation of wellness facilities, a kindergarten, saunas, pools, a nightclub and, notably, an augmentation of our accommodations with additional rooms, chalets and apartments. The next step involved a meeting with the bank, leveraging the Austrian young entrepreneur's subsidised loans to finance this ambitious expansion.

A Comprehensive Approach

One year after the initial opening, construction commenced again. This time, armed with operating plans, budgets, strategic planning and a full-fledged business plan, I embarked on a journey to amplify the dimensions of my dream. The new construction would magnify the hotel, making it four times its original size. It was a leap into uncharted territory, guided not just by youthful enthusiasm but also by meticulous planning and a comprehensive understanding of the challenges and opportunities ahead.

As the chapter unfolded, the expansion became more than a physical augmentation; it was a testament to resilience, adaptability and the ability to glean essential lessons from the initial phase of our endeavour. The journey into growth was not just an architectural expansion but a holistic transformation marked by strategic insight and a deeper understanding of the business landscape.

MARKUS HOFER

Hotel Hofer ALM

CHAPTER 13

Evolving Success – From Hands-On to Team Dynamics

With the expansion successfully realised, the venture entered a new phase where success was not merely gauged by occupancy rates and feel-good elements; it translated into tangible financial gains. As the dimensions of the business grew, so did the complexities, reshaping my role from hands-on involvement to a focus on team management, people leadership, number analysis, planning and budgeting. The connection with our guests underwent a transformation, requiring a shift from direct interaction to a more behind-the-scenes orchestration.

Changing Dynamics

The larger scale and increased guest numbers altered the dynamics of our connection with guests. No longer could it rely solely on my personal engagement; it had to be mediated through the team. The early investment in building a trust bank with my team proved invaluable. The strong friendships cultivated over the years paid dividends as each team member stepped up, ensuring that the vital connection with guests remained intact. The staff became the conduit, a bridge that extended beyond my individual reach.

Team Connection

The connection established with the team during the formative years became a critical asset. The bonds of camaraderie and shared experiences forged a team capable of not only maintaining but also enhancing the guest experience. The connection, once centred around a singular figure, now radiated through a collective effort.

Strength in Numbers

Surprisingly, the expansion didn't amplify the challenges; instead, it simplified the management process. The larger business size became manageable, not because of its sheer scale but due to the robust team that had been meticulously built over the years. Many eyes, ears and hands made the workload lighter. The strong foundation laid during the early stages of the venture now bore fruit, transforming the business into a well-oiled machine where the collective strength of the team propelled us forward.

As the chapter unfolded, the evolution from a hands-on approach to a reliance on team dynamics marked not just a shift in operations but a testament to the enduring value of investing in people. The journey showcased the resilience of a venture grounded in strong team bonds and affirmed that success, in its truest form, is a collective endeavour.

CHAPTER 14

Unveilling Realities - From Dreams to Business Realities

The trajectory of my venture underwent radical changes, mirroring the growth, and not just in size, but in complexity. Two more extensions materialised, and adding more rooms, accommodations, amenities like a nightclub, tennis courts, a children's playground and a third restaurant. The early parts of the building underwent remodelling, integrating new business tools such as a computer and a fax machine (a novelty in the town) and establishing partnerships with additional travel operators.

From Dreams to Realities

The starry-eyed approach of my early venture had given way to a more pragmatic reality. My role had metamorphosed from a hands-on operator to an orchestrator behind the scenes, managing an ever-expanding team. The dream of skiing with guests and friends during the day or engaging in casual conversations at the bar with regular patrons had become a distant memory. Mountain walks were replaced by attendance at tourism board meetings, sessions with accountants and meetings with the bank manager. The idyllic 'happy place' had transformed into a place of business.

Navigating Distances

The distance between my initial dreams and the current reality became palpable. The allure of success and financial gains had steered me away from the carefree life of a ski instructor, introducing me to the demanding role of a businessman. The question loomed: had I inadvertently traded my soul for success? Had I forsaken my left-leaning ideology? These contemplations raised deeper questions about identity and purpose.

Reflecting on the Future

As the worry-free days of being a ski instructor transformed into the complexities of entrepreneurship, the impending arrival of a son brought forth a moment of introspection. Was this the life I envisioned for my child? Did he have a choice in the path his life would take? The impending responsibilities of fatherhood prompted a re-evaluation of priorities and a reconsideration of the future.

A Soul-Searching Moment

The proverb 'Be careful what you ask for, you may get it' reverberated in my mind. The juxtaposition of dreams versus reality stirred a soul-searching journey. The question lingered: What would my future hold, and who would I become? The dichotomy between the pursuit of success and the essence of a meaningful life unfolded, prompting a contemplation of the roads travelled and those yet to be explored.

CHAPTER 15

Down Under Dreams – A Fresh Start in Australia

Australia, etched in my heart with its happy memories and unique way of life, beckoned as a land of opportunities beyond the confines of the Austrian resort I had built. Life had become somewhat restrictive, and the idea of spending the rest of my days tethered to a single business weighed heavily, especially after years of exploring the vastness of the world.

The acceptance of familial assistance, while initially beneficial, had evolved into a complex situation. The demands grew, and the dynamics shifted with the entry of a new family member, my father's new wife, into the partnership. As the allure of Australia beckoned, the decision to sell our resort to a time-share group materialised. The transaction, teetering on the edge at times, ultimately concluded, yielding proceeds substantial enough to settle all debts and, after taxes, leave us with a promising start in Australia.

Now a family of three, with a six-month-old son in tow, a new chapter unfolded. Belongings were packed into a container, unnecessary items were either sold or gifted to friends and we embarked on a journey to a new country. The prospect of migration was daunting, and seeking a franchise with solid support appeared to be a safe pathway. One name resonated strongly – McDonald's. Armed with a recommendation from a family friend who was a McDonald's licensee, we eagerly jetted off to attend an interview at the McDonald's head office in Thornleigh.

The Land of Opportunities

Australia, with its vast landscapes and vibrant culture, offered a canvas for new beginnings. The decision to leave behind the familiar and embrace the unknown underscored the spirit of adventure that had always defined my journey.

McDonald's – A New Chapter

With a recommendation in hand, the prospect of joining the McDonald's franchise promised stability and support in this new venture. The interview at the McDonald's head office marked the initiation of a journey that would unfold in the heart of Sydney, bringing with it fresh challenges, opportunities and the promise of a different kind of success.

An Entrepreneur's Odyssey Continues

As the wheels of change were set in motion, the transition from Austrian entrepreneur to aspiring Australian franchisee marked a turning point. The next chapter in the odyssey would be written in the bustling streets of Sydney, under the iconic golden arches of McDonald's – a symbol of a global enterprise and a fresh start in a new land.

CHAPTER 16

The Golden Arches Beckon – A New Beginning with McDonald's

The first interview at McDonald's felt surreal, stepping into a world vastly different from the alpine landscapes of Tirol, Austria. Clad in attire unfamiliar to the Tyrolean sensibilities, the interview process presented a series of stages, including a three-day stint working in a store alongside an existing licensee. This was a stark departure from the eight years of autonomy, where reporting to someone else was a foreign concept.

The final interview with the board of McDonald's took an unexpected turn for the better. It turned out that Peter Ritchie, the chairman and CEO of McDonald's Australia, was not just a corporate figure but a passionate skier. Whether it was the prospect of a ski buddy or the experiences garnered in the hospitality industry in Austria which paved the way, the details mattered little. What mattered was that I became an 'RA'—a registered applicant. This designation didn't offer much initially, except for the promise of 12 months of McDonald's training ahead, sans pay, sans a guaranteed store offer and uncertainty about the location of our potential store. Yet, it was a step forward—and an opportunity with a well-recognised brand and the promise of support.

Navigating Unfamiliar Territories

The transition from the familiar role of an independent entrepreneur to a prospective franchisee with McDonald's brought forth a whirlwind of changes. Adjusting to a new dress code, following a structured application process and facing the uncertainties of the journey ahead were all part of the challenge.

An Unexpected Connection

The serendipity of encountering a CEO who shared a passion for skiing opened unexpected doors. Whether it was a shared enthusiasm for the slopes or the alignment of values from my hospitality background, the connection proved fortuitous. It was a reminder that, sometimes, personal interests and professional opportunities can intersect in unexpected ways.

RA (Registered Applicant) – A Symbol of Potential:

Being designated as an 'RA' symbolised potential – a potential that would unfold over the next year through rigorous training, learning the intricacies of McDonald's operations and preparing for the responsibilities that lay ahead. The golden arches beckoned, promising not just a business venture but a journey into a globally recognised brand with the backing of a supportive organisation.

CHAPTER 17

Navigating Corporate Realities – A Lesson in Adaptation

The transition from an independent business owner to a franchisee under the McDonald's corporate umbrella brought about a reality I hadn't fully anticipated. I quickly realised that being a part of a renowned global brand also meant being entwined in a structured corporate environment, a stark contrast to the entrepreneurial freedom I had grown accustomed to.

The 'Rap Session' and Unspoken Rules

In the early days, I recall a 'rap session', a forum seemingly designed for open discussion and feedback. However, it didn't take long for me to grasp the unspoken rule – keep your opinions positive and conformist. Any deviation from the narrative of unwavering contentment was met with resistance. It was a quick lesson in corporate culture, where dissenting voices were unwelcome.

Confrontation with authority

A few days later, a summons from Guy Russo, the franchise manager at the time, served as a clear message. I was reminded that conformity was non-negotiable. If I harboured any discontent with the system, my options were simple: adapt or leave. It was a stark introduction to a management style that leaned heavily on fear, intimidation and the assertion of power. As a newcomer to a foreign land with a family to support, the decision to adapt became a pragmatic one.

Silenced Frustration and Unexpected Bonds

While the corporate environment stifled individual expressions of frustration, connecting with fellow 'RAs' undergoing similar experiences became a source of solace. Shared grievances, whispered conversations and subtle nods in acknowledgment became the unspoken language of those navigating the corporate labyrinth. Amidst the stifling atmosphere, friendships were forged during courses and training sessions, enduring beyond the corporate constraints.

Hamburger University and Unlikely Bonds

Attending Hamburger University and other corporate courses, intended to instil adherence to McDonald's standards, unintentionally became a hub for forming connections. It was, in these structured learning environments, that I found camaraderie with like-minded individuals facing similar challenges. The friendships forged during those times proved resilient, extending beyond the confines of corporate mandates.

As I learned to navigate the intricacies of corporate expectations, adaptability became a survival skill and unexpected alliances provided a support system in an environment that often demanded conformity over individual expression.

BECOMING A FRANCHISE.

CHAPTER 18

The Waiting Game – Corporate Chess and a Sydney Store Offer

As the weeks turned into months, the culmination of my McDonald's training approached, marked by the anticipation of a store offer. Yet, this period unfolded as a frustrating waiting game, revealing the intricacies of McDonald's corporate chess.

Corporate Secrecy and Speculation

The veil of secrecy shrouded the allocation process, leaving us – the aspiring franchisees – in a state of speculation and hearsay. Rumours about who would receive what store echoed through the corridors of training centres, creating an atmosphere of uncertainty and intrigue. McDonald's held all the cards, determining the trajectory of our professional lives.

Power Dynamics and Store Allocation Games

The power dynamic was evident – McDonald's controlled the narrative. Store offers were strategically placed, seemingly favouring those with the greatest potential for lucrative sales. The management played a game of secrecy and ambiguity, pitting registered applicants against each other with varying tales. It was a manoeuvre to keep us guessing, ensuring that the company retained the upper hand.

The Rejected Offer and Corporate Displeasure

My first store offer arrived, but its location, a remote country town far from the bustling city life, clashed with my aspirations for family life and personal fulfilment. Rejecting the offer, however, proved to be a transgression in the eyes of McDonald's. The corporate response conveyed an unspoken message: How dare you reject an opportunity that was meant to make you rich? The consequence was clear – I found myself back in the pool of applicants, my rejection seen as an "act of defiance."

Extended Training and the Sydney Store Offer

Another offer emerged 16 months into my McDonald's journey. This time, it was a store in Sydney's eastern suburbs, lacking a drive through – a less-than-ideal proposition. The lessons learned from my previous rejection prompted a different decision. Recognising the importance of settling in Sydney, I accepted the offer, embracing a B-grade store. It was a compromise, but it provided a foothold in the city I desired.

The waiting game, fraught with corporate manoeuvres, power dynamics and unexpected twists, had finally delivered a store offer. Little did I know that this next chapter would immerse me in the challenges and rewards of operating a McDonald's store in the heart of Sydney.

CHAPTER 19

The Sydney Venture – Triumphs, Trials and McDonald's Grading Games

Building a McDonald's store in Maroubra marked a familiar path, leveraging the experience gained in Austria. The process of setting up felt almost routine, and the challenges of hiring and training a team were mitigated by the camaraderie forged with fellow trainee licensees.

Navigating Language Nuances

English as a second language added a layer of complexity to the hiring process. Reading candidates accurately became a nuanced endeavour, and, at times, the outcomes were less than ideal. Yet, the familiar rhythm of opening a store resonated, drawing on the support network cultivated during training.

The Triumph of Maroubra

The grand opening exceeded expectations. Maroubra turned out to be a winning venture, with sales soaring and profitability establishing itself from the outset. However, what seemed like potential support from McDonald's revealed itself as more of a scrutiny – consultant visits turned into marked inspections, recorded meticulously on our files.

Control Through Grading

McDonald's wielded a grading system that, rather than offering support, became a method of control. The frequency of announced and unannounced visits felt more like school inspections than constructive assistance. Consultants, often lacking common sense, subjected us to a subjective evaluation. The consequences were significant, influencing the renewability of our 20-year license. A low mark meant being deemed 'non-expandable,' while a high mark labelled us as 'expandable', opening the door to more store offers.

The Subjectivity of Grading

The game was subjective, with some licensees benefitting from a different set of rules based on their adeptness at playing the system. Incentives offered by licensees, such as invitations to exclusive trips, often influenced the consultant's disposition.

Fortuitously, my skiing background granted me entry into yearly jam sessions in Thredbo, a week-long ski trip with Peter Ritchie, the chairman, and select licensees. Beyond the skiing camaraderie, it became a platform for open discussions and learning from Peter's experiences in bringing McDonald's to Australia.

Seeds of Aspiration

These encounters with Peter sowed seeds of aspiration beyond the role of a glorified manager within a follower-centric system. The yearly sessions in Thredbo not only shaped my understanding of McDonald's intricate workings, but also fuelled a growing desire to think bigger, to transcend the confines of a system designed for conformity. The journey continued, steering towards uncharted territories beyond the golden arches.

CHAPTER 20

Cracks in the Golden Arches – Navigating Existential Questions

As life settled into the rhythm of managing two McDonald's stores and embracing the rewards of financial prosperity, I found myself at a crossroads. A new house in Church Point, nestled amidst the natural beauty of Sydney's northern beaches, bore witness to the expansion of the family, welcoming a daughter into our midst. Luxury additions such as new cars and a ski chalet in Thredbo complemented the financial success brought by operating what many saw as a mere 'burger joint'.

Substantial Rewards, Shallow Fulfilment

The financial rewards of the McDonald's enterprise were undeniably substantial, affording a comfortable lifestyle. Yet, beneath the surface, a growing dissatisfaction emerged. The repetitive nature of managing the business left little room for inspiration or intellectual challenge. The business required adherence to established rules, with little room for entrepreneurial spirit. Operating within the McDonald's system meant being a cog in a well-oiled machine. Whether present or absent, the impact seemed negligible. Doubts began to encroach, and questions about the long game loomed.

An Existential Dilemma

The routine of dealing with juvenile staff and navigating a system designed to exploit an age-based wage system brought forth an existential dilemma. What was the purpose of my role in this system? Could I contribute more? The realisation that, "in the grand scheme," my presence or absence made little difference fuelled a desire for something more meaningful. The financial benefits, though significant, failed to inspire a deeper sense of purpose.

Searching for the Entrepreneurial Spirit

With a growing sense of discontent, the search for a more meaningful path began. The allure of financial success waned, and the desire to make a difference, to contribute in a way that transcended the confines of the McDonald's system, intensified. The quest for the entrepreneurial spirit, creativity unbounded by rigid regulations, took root. The journey ahead, uncertain and uncharted, beckoned. The next chapter awaited, promising challenges and opportunities beyond the golden arches.

CHAPTER 21

A Sip of Inspiration – The Starbucks Revelation

Midway through the 90s, on a ski expedition to Whistler, Canada, I stumbled upon a phenomenon that would alter my perspective on business and fuel a renewed sense of inspiration. In Vancouver, on every street corner, the iconic green logo of Starbucks beckoned. Intrigued, I ventured into a store and discovered a coffee haven that resonated with my European taste – a place that transcended the mundane and embraced a hip, stylish atmosphere.

Starbucks: A Revelation

Starbucks, with its distinctive green cups gracing the hands of every second person on the bustling streets, was a revelation. The business model, the ambiance, the uncomplicated yet sophisticated nature – it all left an indelible mark. Enamoured by this newfound discovery, I immersed myself in the world of Starbucks. I picked up a book by Howard Schultz, the founder and then CEO, in one of the stores, absorbing the tale of how he reinvented the Viennese or Italian coffee shop, making it cool and convenient.

A Call to the Coffee Pioneer

Curiosity piqued, I delved into researching Starbucks. A spark ignited, and a plan formed. I sought out Howard Behar, the International President of Starbucks, wanting to learn more about the company's international expansion plans. Dialling his number was a shot in the dark, but to my surprise, he answered. In a conversation that spanned Australia, Austria and Starbucks, Howard Behar shared insights into the company's global ambitions.

A Spontaneous Visit to Seattle

Seattle, the birthplace of Starbucks, wasn't on my travel itinerary. Yet, fuelled by newfound excitement, I rerouted my journey. A meeting with Howard Behar was arranged at the Starbucks Headquarters in Seattle. Leaving the snowy slopes of Whistler behind, I ventured to the heart of Starbucks to glean insights from a man who played a pivotal role in the brand's international expansion. What awaited was more than just coffee; it was a lesson in innovation, global vision and the art of brewing success, one cup at a time.

CHAPTER 22

The Maestro Behind the Mug – Howard Behar, Starbucks President International

In my quest to understand the essence of Starbucks and its global ambitions, I found myself intrigued not only by the brand but also by the visionary leader steering its international ship – Howard Behar.

The Man Behind the Coffee Empire

Howard Behar's journey is intertwined with the very fabric of Starbucks. Joining the company in 1989, he played a pivotal role in shaping the culture and values that define Starbucks today. His influence extended beyond coffee beans and espresso machines; it permeated the soul of the company, creating an environment that prioritised people over profits.

Leadership Philosophy – Servant Leadership

Howard Behar is not your conventional corporate executive. His leadership philosophy revolves around the concept of 'servant leadership.' Instead of a top-down approach, he championed a model where leaders exist to serve their teams. This ideology infused Starbucks with a unique culture with one that valued every employee and emphasised the importance of human connection in the coffee business.

International Expansion – Nurturing the Global Sip

As President of Starbucks International, Behar played a pivotal role in steering the company into uncharted waters. The expansion beyond North America was a testament to his vision of making Starbucks a global phenomenon. Under his leadership, the brand transitioned from a local coffeehouse to a cultural icon recognised across continents.

A Mentor and Guide

Beyond his corporate responsibilities, Howard Behar became a mentor and guide to many, offering insights into leadership, business and life. His approachability and genuine interest in people made him a respected figure within Starbucks and beyond.

The Meeting in Seattle – A Personal Encounter

My meeting with Howard Behar at the Starbucks Headquarters in Seattle wasn't just about business; it was a dialogue with a man whose passion for coffee was matched only by his commitment to fostering a culture of warmth and belonging. His openness to share the Starbucks story, coupled with a genuine interest in my background, left a lasting impression.

A Sip of Wisdom

Howard Behar's influence extended beyond coffee; it was a sip of wisdom that transcended business realms. From servant leadership to the global expansion of Starbucks, his legacy continues to inspire those who recognise the power of a shared cup of coffee in creating connections that span the globe.

CHAPTER 23

Brewing a Starbucks Empire Down Under

In the quiet hum of coffee beans grinding and the warmth of Howard Behar's mentorship, a venture was born – a joint endeavour to introduce the iconic Starbucks experience to the land Down Under.

Seeds of Collaboration

The collaboration between Starbucks and myself took root after years of discussions, presentations and shared visions. From boardrooms in Hawaii to conversations in the tranquil corners of New Zealand and Howard's home in Seattle, ideas were exchanged, plans were laid and the foundation for Starbucks' expansion into Australia was set.

Navigating the Australian Landscape

Australia posed a unique set of challenges – steep real estate costs, high labour expenses and a coffee culture deeply ingrained in the fabric of society. The scepticism of the Australian public, bordering on arrogance, presented a formidable obstacle. Moreover, the country was already dotted with countless coffee shops, each claiming its own space in the hearts of discerning patrons.

A Strategic Approach

Recognising the hurdles ahead, we crafted a meticulous plan for a slow and organic expansion. The blueprint aimed at establishing five stores in the first five years, with Sydney as the primary focus. This measured approach sought to embed Starbucks into the Australian coffee culture gradually.

Partnership with Purpose

Working alongside Howard Behar was more than a professional collaboration; it was a partnership grounded in shared values and a commitment to authenticity. Our planning sessions were characterised by agreement, a shared ethos and a profound understanding of the challenges and opportunities that lay ahead.

Soaking in Wisdom

The wisdom shared by Howard during these formative stages was invaluable. Drawing from his experiences and insights, I absorbed the essence of Starbucks' success – an unwavering dedication to quality, a commitment to creating a genuine connection with customers and an understanding that, at its core, Starbucks was more than a coffee brand; it was a community.

A Pleasure in Planning

Unlike many endeavours driven by profit margins and aggressive timelines, the planning with Howard Behar was a pleasure. It wasn't just about opening stores; it was about weaving Starbucks into the cultural tapestry of Australia. Each step was measured, intentional and carried the essence of a shared passion for the coffee experience.

CHAPTER 24

Finding Mentorship in the Steam of Coffee

In the aromatic embrace of a coffee cup, I found not just the rich brew of beans but also a mentor who would reshape my perspective on life and business – Howards. His role in Starbucks wasn't just about steering an international coffee empire; it was about infusing the essence of human connection into the very pores of the company.

A Mentorship Beyond Espresso

As I delved into the intricacies of Starbucks, guided by Howard's insights, I discovered that mentorship could transcend the boundaries of business. It wasn't merely about understanding the coffee trade; it was about learning the art of leadership, the importance of fostering a culture of warmth and the magic of genuine human connections.

Connecting the Dots

Behar's teachings were like dots scattered across my life's canvas. From the rebellious spirit of my Steiner-like school days to the immersive experience of ski instructing in the Austrian Alps, there was a common thread – connecting with people. The entrepreneurial spirit cultivated in the Alps found resonance in the coffee-scented air of Starbucks.

From Mountain Slopes to Corporate Halls

The shift from the snow-capped mountains to the corporate halls of McDonald's had initially felt like a departure from the passion-driven life I had known. However, as I sipped on the wisdom shared by Howard, I realised that the entrepreneurial flame need not be extinguished. It could be reignited in unexpected places, much like the aroma of a freshly brewed cup.

The Intersection of Passion and Business

Howards mentorship taught me that passion need not be confined to the slopes of a ski resort or the atmosphere of a coffee shop. It could infuse every aspect of life, including the seemingly mundane corridors of corporate structures. Starbucks, under his influence, was not just a coffee purveyor; it was a community, a global hub where people connected over shared moments and conversations.

The Ripple Effect

As the ripples of Howard's teachings settled within me, I began to view my journey with a new lens. The mountains of Austria, the McDonald's stores in Sydney and the vibrant pulse of Starbucks – they were all interconnected chapters in a narrative fuelled by passion and guided by mentorship.

A Connection Beyond Coffee

In Howard Behar, I found not just a mentor in business but a connection that transcended the world of coffee. His philosophy of servant leadership, his emphasis on genuine human connections and his ability to blend passion with practicality left an indelible mark, challenging me to see the world – and my journey – through a lens of shared experiences and meaningful connections.

CHAPTER 25

Navigating Stormy Waters

The day of signing the Starbucks Australia joint venture marked a turning point, not only in my professional journey but also in the complex world of corporate relationships.

Breaking Ties with McDonald's

Unravelling my ties with McDonald's proved to be more arduous than anticipated. The management's pettiness and jealousy created unnecessary hurdles. Only the intervention of Peter Ritchie, a friend forged through a shared passion for skiing, smoothed the transition. With the McDonald's chapter closed, my focus shifted entirely to the impending venture with Starbucks.

A Bittersweet Signature

The excitement of signing the agreement in Seattle was overshadowed by unexpected news from Howard Behar. This momentous occasion marked his departure from Starbucks, leaving Peter Maslen, a former KFC executive, as his successor. As we engaged in the formalities of signing, Peter's initial words were far from encouraging. He expressed discontent with the deal, preferring a larger company for the joint venture and proposing an aggressive rollout plan of at least 200 stores in the first five years.

An Unsettling Proposal

Peter's objection to the agreed business plan and his preference for a rapid expansion strategy were unsettling. The fast-paced growth he envisioned would dilute my financial stake rapidly, and finding suitable locations for such an ambitious plan in Australia seemed impractical.

Peter Bringing in New Dynamics ... A Fresh Perspective:

The arrival of Peter Masle at Starbucks introduced a new dynamic to our team. With Peter's perspective, it became an opportunity for reflection on the contributions and roles within the project. Although it appeared that my initial input was reassessed, this shift in dynamics encouraged a reevaluation of strategies and contributions. Peter Maslen's involvement, while challenging, provided a stimulus for growth and innovation, pushing me to refine my approach and strengthen my position within the team. It was a reminder that progress often comes from facing and overcoming challenges, turning scrutiny into an opportunity for development.

Under Supportive Guidance:

Adding a layer of support and oversight, Kathy White, a respected Starbucks veteran, was appointed to provide guidance and feedback. Her role was to observe and share insights with the team in Seattle, ensuring that we aligned with corporate standards and goals. Kathy's experience and aspirations brought a valuable perspective to the table, enriching the team's dynamics and fostering a culture of accountability and growth. This environment encouraged me to navigate the corporate landscape with greater awareness and to view challenges as opportunities for personal and professional development.

In the evolving corporate landscape, the guiding principle evolved to strategic diligence. Each decision and action became an opportunity for thoughtful planning and foresight. What started as an exhilarating joint venture journey matured into a voyage through challenging, yet enriching, experiences. This period set the stage for a compelling narrative of personal and professional growth, inviting me to harness my resilience and strategic insight to navigate through complexities and emerge stronger.

CHAPTER 26

Cultivating a Strong Team:

Amidst a backdrop of corporate evolution and dynamic challenges, the importance of forming a cohesive and committed team became clear as the cornerstone of Starbucks' success in Australia. Leveraging my previous experiences, I focused on bringing together individuals who not only resonated with our shared vision but also demonstrated a consistent standard of excellence. This deliberate and thoughtful assembly of talent laid the foundation for a team equipped to thrive and drive our venture forward.

Recruiting Familiar Faces

To anchor the foundation of our Starbucks journey, I brought in Nalin Prakash, an experienced manager from my Maroubra McDonald's store. His familiarity with my expectations and management style made him an invaluable asset. Joining him were other familiar faces like Emma Egan, another former McDonald's employee and Ian McKenzie, a skilled marketing manager with whom I had past connections within the McDonald's system. These were not just hires; they were individuals I knew had my back and would contribute to the atmosphere I aimed to create – a small, aligned team ready to face the challenges ahead.

Strategic Location and Stellar Opening

Securing a prime location for our first store was a strategic move. The new Starbucks store, strategically positioned just before the Sydney Olympics in an AAA location with excellent exposure, was housed in a brand-new building. The groundwork for this location had been laid while I was still in training in Seattle many months prior. Nalin as the store manager was instrumental in building a team largely of his choosing, complemented by support from Ian back at our headquarters in Terry Hills. With Peter Maslen kept at bay in Seattle, we executed a sensational first store opening that surpassed all sales projections, dreams and expectations.

Overcoming Scepticism

The success of the first store was a testament to the magic pull of the Starbucks brand, dispelling any doubts about its viability in Australia. Despite initial scepticism and rumours, our achievements demonstrated that the Starbucks spirit could thrive Down Under. The energy and dedication of our team, many of whom had been part of my previous ventures, generated a positive force that overshadowed any negativity or attempts at sabotage.

Embracing a Moment of Unity:

In a turning point of collaboration, Peter Maslen and I found common ground, inspired by the success of our first store. This achievement offered a moment to reflect and regroup, emphasizing the importance of nurturing a team spirit. I was committed to cultivating a company culture that resonated with the values heralded by Howard Behar—a culture robust enough to embrace internal challenges and enrich the broader Starbucks community.

This initial triumph laid a solid foundation for our journey ahead, opening doors to new opportunities and learnings as we expanded further into the Australian market, continually evolving and strengthening our approach.

CHAPTER 27

Accelerating Growth and Addressing Challenges:

As the Starbucks venture in Australia flourished, the enthusiasm from the board fueled a swift expansion, marked by the launch of numerous stores in rapid succession. This period of accelerated growth brought to light various operational challenges, presenting an opportunity to strengthen our foundation. Addressing these challenges head-on allowed us to refine our processes and systems, ensuring that our expansion was not only fast but also sustainable and aligned with our long-term vision.

Embracing New Opportunities for Growth:

The strategic choice to expedite our expansion unveiled unique opportunities alongside challenges that were unforeseen. Our partnership with global logistics companies, while introducing additional costs, also ensured a consistent Starbucks experience worldwide. Importing high-quality coffee beans from Seattle and embracing global store fit-outs enriched our Australian stores with the authentic Starbucks essence. Adhering to the comprehensive finance and Point of Sale (POS) systems provided by Seattle, despite the complexity and added expense, further aligned us with Starbucks' global standards, enhancing our operational efficiency and customer experience. This phase was a crucial learning curve, allowing us to navigate our growth journey with a focus on quality and global consistency.

Journey Towards Operational Excellence:

The Starbucks stores flourished, capturing the hearts of the Australian market and establishing a new benchmark for excellence. This success was underpinned by a commitment to maintaining the brand's integrity and global standards, through importing high-quality coffee and store components, alongside leveraging the expertise of US-based staff for oversight. These steps, essential for ensuring a consistent Starbucks experience, paved the way for our remarkable achievement: recording the highest average store transactions globally. This milestone, not only celebrated our achievements, but also illuminated the path forward, focusing on enhancing operational efficiencies to support our continued growth and success in the market.

Strategic Focus and Board Engagement:

Peter Maslen, while initially critical of the business plan, brought valuable attention to the importance of profitability and financial sustainability. Our adherence to budgets and cash forecasts highlighted our commitment to fiscal responsibility. This constructive dialogue with the board underscored the evolving nature of the Starbucks venture in Australia, signaling the need for strategic adjustments to ensure long-term success. The focus shifted towards enhancing the venture's sustainability, demonstrating a proactive approach to growth and adaptability in the ever-changing market landscape.

Embracing Evolution and Strategic Transition:

As the Starbucks Australia venture grew and its complexities became more evident, I recognized the importance of adapting to the evolving needs of the operation. With the foundational phase of the rollout successfully completed, it was clear that the next phase might benefit from a leadership style with a more traditional corporate background, contrasting with my entrepreneurial approach. This realization sparked the consideration of a strategic transition that would honor the contributions made and the dedication invested while opening the door to new leadership that could navigate the corporate aspects more naturally.

This period of reflection was not about seeking an exit but about envisioning a future that ensures the continued success of Starbucks in Australia and aligns with my own growth and aspirations as an entrepreneur. It became a moment to assess how best to support the brand's journey forward and define my next steps in a way that reflects both my achievements with Starbucks and my personal entrepreneurial path.

CHAPTER 28

The Evolving Partnership and Strategic Realignment:

Three years into the Starbucks venture, with 29 stores thriving across four states and transaction counts exceeding expectations, we reached a pivotal moment of strategic reflection. The ambition to secure AAA sites for further expansion faced practical challenges, highlighting the need for adaptability in our growth strategy. This juncture brought about a meaningful dialogue between Peter Maslen and myself, focusing on reconciling the aspiration for rapid expansion with the reality of the market's availability of prime locations. It was an opportunity for strategic realignment, ensuring that our vision for Starbucks in

Australia remained robust and responsive to the evolving landscape.

Operational Success and Strategic Expansion:

The operational success of our stores marked a significant achievement in our journey. The investment in a dedicated support team to facilitate rapid expansion and the capital directed towards new locations were crucial steps in scaling our presence. As we looked to further our growth, the challenge of aligning our ambitious expansion plans with the availability of prime locations became apparent. This situation prompted a strategic reassessment, focusing on how to sustain our growth momentum while adapting to the realities of the market. It was an opportunity to refine our expansion strategy, ensuring that our journey forward was both ambitious and grounded in practical considerations.

Strategic Transition and Collaborative Decision-Making:

In recognizing the evolution of the Starbucks Australia venture and the need for new leadership to navigate its next phase, a collaborative decision was made for me to embark on new opportunities. This decision emerged from thoughtful discussions, reflecting a shared commitment to the venture's ongoing success and an appreciation for the contributions made. The process of defining the terms of this transition was approached with careful consideration and negotiation, ensuring a resolution that was mutually beneficial and respectful. This strategic shift marked a positive and forward-looking conclusion to my involvement, setting the stage for new leadership to steer Starbucks Australia toward its bright future.

A Constructive Transition:

As the transition unfolded, the distinct differences in management styles between Peter Maslen and the inspirational Howard Behar highlighted the diverse approaches within the corporate world. This period of change served as a valuable learning experience, reinforcing my understanding and appreciation for the variety of leadership philosophies. It underscored my entrepreneurial spirit's drive for innovation and adaptability, affirming my path towards ventures that align more closely with my personal values and approach to business. This realization marked not an end, but a new beginning, rich with potential for growth and new opportunities.

Embarking on a New Journey:

The conclusion of my time with the corporate world marked a pivotal moment, heralding the start of an exciting new chapter in my life. Equipped with invaluable experiences, insightful lessons, and strengthened resilience, I eagerly anticipated the array of opportunities that lay ahead. In the years that followed, Starbucks Australia experienced several leadership transitions, reflecting the dynamic nature of the business. The ambitious growth strategy pursued after my departure led to the launch of many new stores, showcasing a commitment to expansion. This period of rapid growth underscored the challenges and compromises inherent in scaling at such a pace, highlighting the importance of strategic decision-making in business development.

Reflective Insights from Continued Growth:

Witnessing the evolution of Starbucks Australia following my departure offered a unique perspective on the outcomes of various strategic decisions, particularly regarding the expansion and subsequent store closures. While it's natural to feel a complex mix of emotions during such transitions, the predominant feeling was one of reflective learning rather than schadenfreude. Observing these developments reinforced the importance of strategic foresight and adaptability, underscoring the lessons learned during my tenure. As I moved forward from this chapter in my entrepreneurial journey, these insights became integral to shaping my future endeavors, contributing to a deeper understanding of business dynamics and personal growth.

CHAPTER 29

Reflecting on Starbucks, Passion Persists Taking a Break

Parting ways with Starbucks marked a significant shift – from the intensity of corporate life to a seemingly abrupt nothingness. Having consistently placed business at the centre of my life, with minimal room for external pleasures, this juncture prompted reflection on what would truly fulfil me in the uncertain future.

Family Time and Ski Trips

Amidst the business-centric lifestyle, family time and ski trips had always been non-negotiable priorities. Skiing provided not just a recreational outlet but a shared experience, creating lasting memories. However, as events unfolded, it became evident that these pursuits – while cherished – were insufficient to sustain my marriage.

Media Misinterpretations

As media outlets began speculating on the closure of Starbucks stores in Australia, a wave of misinformation and misguided assumptions swept through social platforms, newspapers and YouTube videos. The supposed experts, lacking factual insights, offered inaccurate analyses. The reasons for the store closures were misconstrued, overshadowing the brand's success and acceptance in the Australian market.

Starbucks Success and Brand Acceptance

Contrary to the misconceptions propagated by the media, Starbucks has experienced success in Australia. Store transaction counts were robust, the brand resonated with consumers and the coffee received positive reviews. However, the narrative of failure gained traction, perpetuating inaccuracies about the reasons behind the closures.

Learning from Strategic Adjustments:

The decision to close certain stores was a strategic response to the unique challenges of adapting an American business model to the Australian market. These actions highlighted the importance of local market understanding and the need for flexibility in global strategies. The adjustments made were not indicative of the Australian market's lack of potential but rather an opportunity to refine and improve operational approaches. This experience underscored the value of learning from each phase of expansion and the continuous pursuit of alignment between global visions and local realities.

Ongoing Passion for Starbucks

Despite the professional separation, my passion for the Starbucks brand endured. Holding a significant stake in the publicly listed U.S. company, I continued to express confidence in the brand's potential. This chapter's conclusion marked not just the end of a professional journey but the continuation of a personal affinity for a brand that had been a significant part of my entrepreneurial endeavours.

CHAPTER 30

Rediscovering Purpose in a Beachside Gem Loss of Purpose and the Quest for Something More

The aftermath of parting ways with Starbucks brought a sense of aimlessness. The absence of a significant project to delve into left a void. Corporate life, with its structured routines and responsibilities, had been left behind, and the challenge was to find a new venture that resonated with personal aspirations.

Embracing the Small Business Appeal

The desire to avoid corporate entanglements led to a preference for a small business venture. The perfect opportunity presented itself

– a charming café in an enviable location on Balmoral Beach in Mosman, an affluent suburb. The café, exquisitely designed by Mark Landini, exuded the kind of energy that aligned with personal taste.

Seamless Acquisition and Hands-On Management

In a twist of fate, the café was swiftly acquired, making the transition from the corporate world to the intimate setting of a beachside café seamless. Despite inheriting a fantastic team, the café manager's absence on the day of handover necessitated a hands-on approach, stepping back into a familiar role.

Rediscovering Joy in a Small Team

Operating a single café, modest in size but rich in character, proved to be a refreshing change. The small team setting facilitated quick and meaningful connections. Bonds with customers deepened swiftly, leading to the formation of new friendships. The close-knit community in Mosman provided an inspiring backdrop.

Leading from the Front

Being back in a smaller, more intimate team allowed for a return to hands-on leadership, a stark contrast to the restrictive nature of corporate roles. The joy derived from leading from the front, actively engaging with both the team and customers, was reminiscent of earlier experiences.

Profitability and Moments of Contentment

The café, strategically located with captivating beach views, proved to be not only personally fulfilling but also a financially lucrative venture. In this moment, life felt good – contentment found in the simplicity of running a profitable business, fostering connections and revelling in the beachside atmosphere.

The Persistent Urge for More

While the café provided a gratifying chapter, the ever-present urge to embark on new challenges lingered in the background. Despite the current fulfilment, the desire to do more and explore additional avenues continued to shape the evolving journey.

CHAPTER 31

Embracing Flow and Intuition
The Unfolding Philosophy

As more ventures graced the timeline of my professional journey, a subtle philosophy began to crystallise – one anchored in the idea that if something is meant to be, it will unfold effortlessly. This perspective advocated for a balance between ambition and allowing things to take their natural course.

The Art of Non-forcing

In the tapestry of entrepreneurial endeavours, there's an art to not pushing too hard. Recognising that relentless striving doesn't always yield the best outcomes, I learned to let the rhythm of events play out. Sometimes, the most meaningful achievements come when one is attuned to the natural flow of circumstances.

Synchronicity and Meaningful Coincidences

The concept of synchronicity gained prominence—a belief that events are interconnected in meaningful ways, beyond mere chance. A venture's success or a fortuitous encounter wasn't solely a result of meticulous planning; it was often intertwined with a series of serendipitous moments, creating a richer narrative.

Cautious Desires

The proverb 'Be careful what you ask for; you may get it' echoed louder. It underscored the importance of mindful desires – wishing for endeavours aligned with one's values and aspirations. Success, when aligned with genuine goals, tends to bring fulfilment that transcends mere achievement.

The Unseen Dimensions of Business

Beyond the tangible metrics of business success, another dimension emerged – intuition. It became a guiding force alongside facts and figures. The ability to sense the right direction, make decisions based on a deeper understanding and navigate uncertainties with an intuitive compass added a nuanced layer to entrepreneurial ventures.

Trusting the Unseen Forces

Trusting the unseen forces at play in the business landscape became a valuable skill. While data-driven decisions had their place, intuition served as a compass in uncharted territories. It guided through uncertainties, offering insights beyond the scope of conventional analysis.

The Subtle Dance with Destiny

In reflection, the journey began to resemble a subtle dance with destiny. Each venture, with its unique twists and turns, unfolded with a rhythm of its own. The key lay in harmonising with this rhythm, embracing the nuances and learning to navigate the unexpected.

Lessons from the Journey

Through these realisations, the journey taught profound lessons about the delicate balance between ambition and surrender, the interconnectedness of events and the wisdom in allowing the unfolding of one's path. The entrepreneur's journey, it seemed, was as much a dance with fate as it was a strategic pursuit.

CHAPTER 32

A Byron Bay Brew – Blending Business with Bohemia The Unforeseen Call

A seemingly innocuous phone call in early 1992, from an agent echoed the tantalising promise of Byron Bay – a place I had initially dismissed for Starbucks but now presented itself as a canvas for a different kind of venture. The allure of an AAA site beckoned, and so began a journey into the heart of Byron.

Scouting with New Eyes

Setting foot in Byron Bay without the Starbucks lens, I encountered a town pulsating with soul. It wasn't just a location; it was a community ardently resisting the homogenization of global brands, striving to preserve its eclectic, hippie spirit.

Nostalgia and New Beginnings

The town's aura resonated with memories of the 70s, my school days, and the era of free-spirited living. It was a confluence of nostalgia and fresh possibilities. Byron Bay became more than a potential business location; it became a beckoning embrace.

A Pivotal Partner

With the tendrils of my life still firmly entwined in Sydney's schooling system, a move to Byron wasn't an immediate prospect. However, a serendipitous reunion with a former Starbucks team member who dwelled nearby breathed life into the vision – a hands-on partner ready to intertwine their journey with mine.

The Hippie Haven

As the café/restaurant deal materialised, we found ourselves not just buying a business but stepping into the custodianship of an icon in Byron Bay. It wasn't merely a commercial venture; it was an ode to the bohemian heartbeat of this coastal haven.

Community Fusion

Byron Bay, for all its scenic allure, thrived on community values. Our foray into this venture was more than a business transaction; it was a commitment to intertwine with the heartbeat of the town, contributing to its unique ethos.

Navigating Local Sensitivities

The decision to maintain the icon came with its own set of challenges. Byron Bay's locals, proud custodians of their town's identity, were watchful. Navigating the balance between evolution and preservation became a delicate dance – one I was eager to perform with finesse.

The Byron Brew

My Byron Bay venture was a brew of old-world charm, local vibrancy and a pinch of entrepreneurial spirit. It was about savouring the flavours of a community woven into the tapestry of time, respecting its history while crafting a new chapter.

Learning from Byron

In the golden hues of Byron's sunsets, we found not just a business venture but a lesson – an understanding that success here wasn't solely defined by profit margins but by the richness of relationships, the tapestry of community and the authenticity of shared stories.

Byron's Gift

As I embarked on this journey, Byron Bay unfolded its gifts – friendships forged in coastal breezes, conversations that meandered like the waves and the warmth of a community that embraced us not merely as business owners but as custodians of its spirit. The Byron Bay brew, with its distinct notes of bohemia, became a venture fuelled not just by commerce but by the heartfelt symphony of a community dancing to its own rhythm.

CHAPTER 33

Navigating Stormy Seas – A Journey Through Personal Turbulence A Tale of Two Cafés

As the symphony of Byron Bay's bohemian charm played on, another note joined the melody – Utopia Café in Bangalow, a place adorned with style, class and a loyal following. Its acquisition swiftly unfolded. With Michael and Ross, the two visionaries behind Utopia, handing over their legacy, the delicate task of maintaining its essence while enhancing profitability lay ahead.

Two Bases, One Vision

With a café in Byron Bay and another in Bangalow, the dance between two coastal havens intensified. Sydney's café was relinquished, not entirely by choice but by the challenging tides of lease negotiations and a landlord's eagerness to dabble in the world of cafés. The move marked a significant shift – focusing energies on the tranquil embrace of Byron and Bangalow.

Cracks in the Partnership

Yet, as the sun painted the horizon with hues of gold, cracks started to appear in the partnership managing these establishments. Unbeknownst and unforeseen, the journey took an unexpected turn. Negative energies, unforeseen splits with business partners and the weight of navigating through murky waters began to cast dark clouds over the horizon.

A Mental Tempest

Navigating uncharted territories, the mental tempest gathered strength. Unexpected challenges and encounters with negativity took their toll. A partner's departure in Byron, coupled with a sudden break down, ushered in a humbling experience. Life, unpredictable and relentless, thrust me into a realm of unpreparedness – a journey through storms within.

Seeking Sanctuary in Byron

Amid the tumult, the tranquillity of Byron Bay beckoned. Priorities shifted, as personal changes rippled through – marriages ended, and love, unfamiliar in its depth, graced my path. Family support in Australia, while present, took a form not entirely aligned with the solace needed. Byron Bay, a sanctuary in its calm, became a place of retreat, reflection and rejuvenation.

Rediscovering Strength

Amid the ruins of what once was, a guiding light emerged. A newfound understanding of relationships, mindfulness and tolerance ushered in a different chapter. Meeting a love that transcended the familiar contours of life, I rediscovered a strength, not just in resilience but in the transformative power of embracing change.

The Ever-changing Tide

Life's tide, relentless and ever-changing, taught lessons unscripted. Through the ebb and flow, from stormy seas to tranquil shores, the journey carved its indelible marks – a narrative woven with threads of personal evolution, the resilience of the human spirit and the untold stories of a life navigating its way through uncharted waters.

CHAPTER 34

The Ripple Effect – Embracing the Power of Positive Leadership Cultivating a Positive Ecosystem

In the intricate dance of life and business, the company we keep shapes not only our journey but also the collective narrative of shared experiences. A chapter dedicated to the profound impact of fostering a positive, supportive environment – an ecosystem where individuals flourish, not just as professionals but as human beings.

The Manager's Role

As the conductor orchestrates a symphony, a manager wields a transformative baton in the workplace. The lessons etched into the fabric of my journey underscore the influential role of a manager in shaping destinies, not merely in the professional realm but echoing into the personal tapestry of each team member.

Creating Success Stories

The power to set the stage for triumph lies within the manager's hands. A leader's true measure lies not merely in the bottom line but in the narratives of success crafted under their watch. A positive influence, a guiding force, a manager can be the wind beneath the wings of their team, propelling them to unforeseen heights.

Each Life Matters

In the hustle of deadlines and quotas, it's easy to lose sight of the human element. Yet, the truth resounds – each life within an organisation matters. Beyond the balance sheets, there exists a realm where individuals navigate the intricate landscape of personal and professional challenges. A manager's actions resonate in this delicate balance.

Managerial Alchemy

The alchemy of leadership lies not in wielding authority but in inspiring greatness. Nurturing an environment where team members feel supported, valued and motivated is the hallmark of effective leadership. The ripples of such leadership extend far beyond office walls, permeating the very fabric of personal lives.

Setting Up for Success

A manager, in essence, is a custodian of potential. The art lies in identifying, harnessing and channelling that potential towards success. Through mentorship, encouragement and genuine care, a manager sets the stage for a collective journey where individual victories resonate as a harmonious melody.

The Ripple Effect

Just as a stone creates ripples upon touching water, a manager's influence extends beyond the immediate. The ripple effect of positive leadership cascades through the professional and personal realms of team members, shaping not only their career trajectories but also the overall quality of their lives.

The Essence of Leadership

In essence, this chapter is a tribute to the unsung heroes – the leaders who recognise that their actions are not confined to the boardroom but reverberate in the hearts and minds of those they lead. An exploration of the transformative power inherent in being a beacon of positivity, support and genuine leadership in the ever-evolving tapestry of life.

CHAPTER 35

**Beyond the Balance Sheet –
The Human Factor in Business
Transactions Unravelling
the Human Thread**

As the ink dries on contracts and the keys to a new venture change hands, a crucial oversight often persists – the human factor. Amidst the stacks of financial statements, projections and business plans, the heartbeat of any enterprise lies in its people. This chapter unfolds the recurrent pattern observed in the intricate dance of buying and selling businesses – the neglect of the intangible but invaluable asset, the team.

The Standard Script

Prospective buyers, armed with calculators and keen eyes for financial nuances, often recite a standard script. 'We like what we see; we won't change anything'. Yet, beneath these well-intentioned assurances lies a frequently missed chapter – the story of the team. A team that, through dedication and collective effort, has contributed to the very success the buyer seeks to acquire.

The Unspoken Change

Despite the promises of continuity, new owners frequently embark on a journey of marking their territory. Changes, whether essential or merely reflective of personal inclinations, send a message – an inadvertent declaration that the existing way was flawed. The unintentional impact on morale reverberates through the ranks, often leading to an exodus of the very talent that fuelled the business's success in the first place.

The Silent Drain

In the aftermath of such transitions, a common theme emerges – a drain on the business's biggest asset, the experienced and committed team. The departure of these individuals, who held the institutional knowledge and intrinsic understanding of the operation, leaves a void that financial figures cannot fill. The collateral damage inflicted on morale and operational efficiency becomes an unaccounted cost.

A Trail of Unravelled Ventures

The narrative takes an introspective turn, reflecting on the fate of businesses post-sale. From the Coogee Beach McDonald's store to the Hotel in Austria, the Mosman Café and even Byron Fresh – all once-vibrant enterprises, their lustre faded as the human touch, the very essence of their success was unintentionally neglected.

The Real Question – What Did They Buy?

Beyond the glossy reports and profit margins, the question lingers – what did the new owners truly acquire? Did they secure a mere brick-and-mortar entity, or did they inherit a living, breathing organism nurtured by a committed team? The recurring theme suggests that the businesses' lifelines were inadvertently severed, resulting in outcomes ranging from financial insolvency to a rapid decline in vibrancy.

Lessons Learned – The Human Element Prevails

This chapter serves as a poignant reminder that beyond the numbers, contracts and physical assets, the soul of a business resides in its people. A call to prospective buyers to not merely peruse the balance sheets but to engage with the beating heart of the enterprise – the dedicated individuals who shape its destiny. A testament to the often-neglected truth that success in business is not solely measured in profits but in the strength and unity of the team propelling it forward.

CHAPTER 36

**The Eroding Essence –
When Business Loses Its Soul
A Common Tale Unfolds**

The chapters in the book of business transitions seem to echo a familiar refrain. A new owner steps into the realm of a once-vibrant enterprise, and with each footfall, a subtle erosion begins – a silent retreat of the very essence that made the business thrive.

The Sequence of Decay

The predictable narrative unfolds. Staff, once the lifeblood of the establishment, exit the stage. With their departure, a palpable vibrancy dissipates. The ebb and flow of daily operations undergoes a subtle shift. Sales, once robust, commence a gradual decline. The reasons, often attributed to external factors, disguise the internal unravelling.

Cost-cutting Initiatives

In an attempt to staunch the bleeding balance sheets, the new custodians initiate a series of cost-cutting measures. Labour costs bear the initial brunt, followed by successive incisions into maintenance and repair budgets. A regime of saving sweeps through the establishment like a winter chill, numbing the warmth that once characterised the business.

The Domino Effect

The repercussions resonate throughout the organisation. The burden of diminished resources weighs heavily on the shoulders of those who remain. A cloud of discontent hovers over the once-thriving community of staff and the customers, sensing the shift in ambiance and finding solace elsewhere.

Culprits of Decline

Amidst the tumult, a familiar pattern emerges – an inclination to lay blame on external factors. Weather conditions, economic climates, interest rates – all become convenient scapegoats. Yet, the true culprit often lies within – an erosion of the business's very soul, the spirit that once propelled it forward.

The Unhappy Symphony

As pressure mounts, a dissonant symphony echoes through the corridors of the business. Unhappy owners, burdened by the weight of unmet expectations, exude a negative energy that permeates every aspect of the establishment. The blame game ensues, with fingers pointing in all directions but towards the core issue – the business has lost its soul.

The Unseen Decline

Amidst the finger-pointing and externalised blame, the internal decline continues its insidious march. What was once a dynamic, spirited enterprise transforms into a mere shell of its former self. The energetic pulse that drew in both customers and staff weakens, leaving a void that cannot be filled by mere financial interventions.

The Lesson in Reflection

This chapter serves as a reflective pause – a reminder that the decline of a business often transcends the externalities used to rationalise its descent. Beyond the balance sheets and operational logistics, lies an intangible yet invaluable element – the soul of the business. As it fades, so does the vitality that once defined it, leaving in its wake a shell yearning to rediscover the essence it lost.

CHAPTER 37

The Power of Positive Energy in Business Success

In the dynamic realm of business, where strategies, innovation and market dynamics play pivotal roles, there exists a subtle yet transformative force that often goes unnoticed – positive energy. It is a force that emanates from every facet of a business, weaving its way through the design, construction, location and – perhaps most importantly – the individuals who breathe life into the organisation.

1. Design and Architecture:

The physical manifestation of positive energy within a business starts with its design and architecture. A thoughtfully crafted space, adorned with elements that inspire creativity, collaboration and a sense of well-being, sets the stage for a positive working environment. The interplay of colours, natural light and open spaces can significantly impact the mood and energy of those within. A design that nurtures a harmonious atmosphere fosters a collective sense of purpose and pride.

2. Building for Success:

The very structure that houses a business carries its own energy. A building constructed with sustainability and environmental consciousness not only aligns with global trends but also contributes positively to the ethos of the organisation. Energy-efficient spaces and a commitment to eco-friendly practices resonate with the modern consumer and, in turn, infuse the business with a sense of responsibility and forward-thinking.

3. Location, Location, Location:

The choice of location is a critical factor in determining the energy a business exudes. A strategic location that aligns with the brand's values and aspirations can attract like-minded individuals and customers. Proximity to nature, cultural hubs, or dynamic urban landscapes can infuse a business with the energy of its surroundings, creating an environment that inspires growth and creativity.

4. The Heartbeat of the Business – Its People:

Perhaps the most influential source of positive energy within a business emanates from the individuals who make up its collective soul. The attitudes, motivations and interactions of employees create a ripple effect throughout the organisation. A workplace culture that fosters camaraderie, encourages innovation and values each individual's contribution generates a positive energy flow that propels the business towards success.

Leadership plays a pivotal role in shaping this positive energy. Leaders who embody optimism, resilience and a forward-thinking mindset set the tone for the entire organisation. Their ability to inspire and motivate creates a culture where challenges are viewed as opportunities, fostering an environment where positive energy becomes a driving force behind success.

In conclusion, the importance of positive energy within a business cannot be overstated. It is a silent yet powerful force that flows through the design, construction, location and, most significantly, the people within the organisation. Recognising and harnessing this energy is not just a choice; it is a strategic imperative for businesses aiming not only to survive but also to thrive in an ever-evolving landscape. As businesses embrace the holistic impact of positive energy, they unlock the potential for enduring success and a legacy that extends far beyond the balance sheet.

CHAPTER 38

**The Symphony of Leadership
- Orchestrating Success
with Harmony**

Leading a team shares a striking resemblance to conducting an orchestra – a delicate dance of coordination, timing and harmony. In this chapter, we explore the analogy of leadership as a conductor, always one beat ahead, setting the stage for success rather than failure. It delves into the principles of hiring the best, empowering through support, fostering continuous learning and the profound impact of acknowledging that happy staff is not just a sentiment but a strategic business advantage.

The Conductor's Beat – Leading with Vision

As a leader, being a beat ahead is akin to having a clear vision. This section explores the importance of setting the direction for the team, aligning goals and providing a roadmap for success. It emphasises that effective leadership is about creating an environment where each team member understands their role in the larger orchestration, contributing to a symphony of collective achievement.

Set Up for Success, Not Failure

The true mark of leadership lies in how well a leader sets their team up for success. This chapter delves into the art of positioning team members in roles that leverage their strengths, fostering an environment where success is not just encouraged but practically inevitable. It explores the role of a leader in removing obstacles and providing the necessary resources for the team to excel.

Empowering Excellence – Hiring the Best and Getting Out of Their Way

The analogy of a conductor hiring virtuoso musicians holds true in the business realm.

This section advocates for hiring the best talent and entrusting them with the autonomy to excel. It explores the concept of leadership as a supportive force, allowing team members the freedom to showcase their skills, innovate and contribute meaningfully to the collective performance.

The Art of Non-intrusive Leadership

Micromanagement, like discordant notes in an orchestra, can disrupt the flow of a team. This chapter delves into the principle of non-intrusive leadership, recognising when to step back and allow capable individuals to execute their roles. It explores how a leader's trust can empower team members to take ownership of their responsibilities, fostering a culture of accountability and self-motivation.

Supportive Leadership – Nurturing Growth and Learning

Leadership extends beyond the operational aspects; it's about supporting the personal and professional growth of the team. This section explores the role of a leader in providing mentorship, resources and opportunities for continuous learning. It emphasises that a thriving team is one where individuals feel valued, supported and equipped to enhance their skills.

The Collective Symphony – Team Collaboration

In the world of leadership, the term 'we' holds more power than 'I'. This chapter delves into the importance of speaking as a team, acknowledging that the achievements of the collective are greater than the sum of individual contributions. It explores the humility of a leader who refrains from taking sole credit, recognising that success is a shared endeavour.

Listening as a Virtue – Addressing Concerns and Encouraging Dialogue

A leader's role extends beyond talking; it involves active listening. This section explores the importance of creating an open dialogue where team members feel heard. It emphasises that addressing concerns, seeking feedback and fostering open communication contribute to a culture of trust, transparency and continuous improvement.

Beyond Business – Integrating Personal Lives

Contrary to the conventional wisdom of keeping personal and professional lives separate, this chapter challenges the notion. It explores the idea that acknowledging and understanding the personal aspects of team members fosters a more compassionate and empathetic workplace. It advocates for a leadership approach that values the whole person, recognising that a content and fulfilled individual contributes positively to the team and, by extension, the business.

Happy Staff, Sound Business Sense

The chapter concludes by reinforcing the notion that happy staff isn't just a feel-good sentiment; but it makes sound business sense. It explores how a positive work environment, where individuals feel valued, supported and engaged, contributes to increased productivity, creativity and overall team satisfaction. It underlines that the success of a business is intricately tied to the happiness and well-being of its staff.

As we conclude this symphony of leadership, the chapters that follow will continue to explore practical strategies, real-world examples and insights into the multifaceted journey of leading a team. The orchestration of success is an ongoing endeavour, and the melody of effective leadership is crafted with a nuanced understanding of people, dynamics and the harmonious blend of professional and personal elements.

CHAPTER 39

Harmonising the Symphony of Change A Move to Simplicity

The ongoing odyssey takes an inward turn, seeking simplicity amidst the complexities of business and life. The Bangalow café finds a new custodian as the decision to sell aligns with the quest for harmony and alignment of purpose.

Full-time Byron Residence

Byron Bay, once a haven, now transforms into a permanent residence. The shift is not merely geographical but emblematic of a commitment to embrace life's ebb and flow in a coastal cocoon.

Navigating Business Partnerships

Yet, even in the serenity of Byron, the tribulations of business persist. A new business partner enters the stage, and the partnership script takes unexpected turns. Motivations clash, and the dissonance of differing objectives reverberates through the business's daily symphony.

Financially Driven Intentions

The new partner's arrival signals a paradigm shift. Financial aspirations eclipse a holistic vision for the business. The enterprise, once a tapestry woven with passion and purpose, risks being reduced to a mere transactional conduit.

Business as a Financial Tool

For the new partner, the business becomes a financial tool – an entity to extract benefits and serve personal financial agendas. The philosophy of business as a vehicle for personal gain diverges sharply from my belief in a business's role as a community pillar and a source of shared prosperity.

Conflicting Management Styles

The clash of management styles becomes palpable. One envisions a business that reinvests, nurtures and grows organically. The other perceives it as an entertainment venue – a stage for showcasing financial prowess without the commitment to nurture its roots.

Impact on the Team

The repercussions ripple through the team. Conflicting messages create confusion, and the staff finds itself caught in the crossfire of dissimilar management approaches. Visits from the absentee partner only compound the issue, injecting negativity into the business's rhythm at its busiest crescendos.

The Struggle for Harmony

The struggle for harmony unfolds not just in the business dynamics but in the interpersonal relationships steering the enterprise. As the dissonance reaches its zenith, the quest for alignment becomes paramount, a melody yet to be composed.

Lessons in Partnerships

This chapter in the narrative illuminates the intricate dance of partnerships – a delicate choreography where each step must harmonise with the other. The lesson learned is etched in the tumultuous cadence of conflicting motives – a reminder that partnerships, like symphonies, thrive when orchestrated with a shared purpose, a commitment to nurture and an understanding that the essence of the business extends beyond financial transactions.

CHAPTER 40

Navigating the Complex Landscape of Partnerships

In the entrepreneurial journey, the allure of partnerships often promises a synergy of strengths, a shared vision and the pooling of diverse talents. However, this chapter explores the intricate challenges that can arise within partnerships – challenges rooted in divergent goals, conflicting objectives, disparate styles, design clashes, distinct personalities and the delicate dance of compromise. To ensure the success of any partnership, a business must ultimately find its way through this intricate web and align itself with a clear vision and decisive execution.

The Mirage of Alignment – Unravelling Different Goals and Objectives

Partnerships often begin with a shared dream, but over time, the divergence in individual goals and objectives can become apparent. Misalignment in long-term visions and strategic objectives can lead to internal friction, slowing down progress and hindering the realisation of collective aspirations. The challenge lies in navigating these differences and fostering a shared understanding of the overarching mission that transcends individual goals.

Clash of Styles – Balancing Design and Operational Approaches

Diverse styles, both in terms of design and operational methodologies, can inject vitality into a partnership. However, when these differences become pronounced, conflicts may arise. A clash of design ideas can create discord in branding, marketing and product development. Striking a balance between individual styles while maintaining a cohesive and recognisable identity becomes essential to prevent dilution and confusion in the eyes of the consumer.

Personality Dynamics – The Human Element of Partnerships

The human factor is perhaps the most unpredictable element in any partnership. Different personalities bring unique perspectives, but they can also be sources of friction. Varied communication styles, decision-making preferences and approaches to problem-solving may result in misunderstandings. Navigating the human dynamics of a partnership requires emotional intelligence, effective communication and a commitment to finding common ground amid diverse personalities.

The Compromise Conundrum – Striking a Balance

Compromise is a cornerstone of successful partnerships, but an excess of compromises can lead to a diluted vision and a sense of dissatisfaction among partners. The delicate art of compromise involves distinguishing between negotiable and non-negotiable elements, fostering open communication to find mutually agreeable solutions and ensuring that each party feels heard and valued.

Vision and Execution – The North Star of Partnership Success

In the face of these challenges, partnerships must find solace and direction in a clear and shared vision. A well-defined vision becomes the guiding force that transcends individual differences, aligning partners towards a common goal. Execution, too, must be decisive and strategic, ensuring that the collective efforts of the partnership are directed towards achieving tangible and meaningful outcomes.

Thriving Amidst Complexity

Partnerships, while laden with challenges, have the potential to transcend individual limitations and achieve greatness. Success lies not in the absence of differences but in the ability to navigate and leverage them to create a more robust and resilient entity. A business, forged through the crucible of diverse goals, conflicting styles and unique personalities, can emerge stronger, with a clear vision that guides its trajectory and an execution plan that propels it towards lasting success. In the ever-changing landscape of partnerships, the journey is not always easy, but the rewards for those who navigate the complexities with resilience and determination can be truly extraordinary.

CHAPTER 41

The Symphony of Renewal
The Aging Business

As the Byron business matured, signs of aging became apparent. To breathe new life into the establishment, the decision for a renewal and redesign was made. The task ahead was monumental – a complete renovation and transformation within a tight timeframe.

A Vision for Transformation

The vision was bold, and the mission clear – to revitalise the business, infuse it with fresh energy and create an ambiance that resonated with both locals and visitors. The importance of this renewal transcended aesthetics; it was a strategic move to secure the business's future.

A Team United

Executing such a vision required an extraordinary effort. The team at Byron Fresh, inspired by a sense of ownership and camaraderie, rallied together. Their commitment to the business, fostered through shared experiences and a culture of belonging, became the driving force behind the ambitious renovation project.

The Impossible Achieved

The timeline set for the renovation was challenging, but the collective determination made the seemingly impossible achievable. Working with two teams around the clock, the business underwent a complete makeover in just 16 days. It was a testament to the team's dedication, resilience and their belief in the importance of their shared endeavour.

Results Beyond Aesthetics

The transformation was not merely cosmetic; it had profound effects on the business dynamics. Sales and profits experienced an upswing, and the revitalised atmosphere created a buzz in Byron Bay. The renewed aesthetic appeal of the establishment aligned seamlessly with the vibrant spirit of the community.

Discontent Amidst Triumph

While the results were cause for celebration, not everyone shared in the jubilation. The business partner, absent during this crucial period, found discontent in the allocation of funds towards the renewal. Yet, the decision to reinvest and enhance the business's appeal would prove to be a fortuitous one.

Financial Stability Amidst Discontent

The discontentment of the business partner, driven by financial motives, contrasted with the business's newfound stability. The ability to set aside funds for unforeseen circumstances became a financial buffer. Howard Behar's wisdom, echoing the perils of operating under financial pressure, resonated as a guiding principle.

Shifting Energies

The renewal was not confined to the physical space; it catalysed a shift in energies. The business, once burdened by the weight of aging infrastructure, now stood rejuvenated, a testament to the belief that investing in and improving the business is an investment in its sustainable future.

The Symphony of Success

This chapter underscores the transformative power of renewal and reinvestment. It illustrates how a united team, fuelled by a shared sense of purpose and a commitment to excellence, can orchestrate success even in the face of challenges. The symphony of renewal, played by the team at Byron Fresh, echoes the timeless truth that investing in the future ensures the continuity of a harmonious business melody.**

CHAPTER 42

The Lifeline of Success – The Imperative of Reinvestment in Your Business

In the dynamic ecosystem of business, the concept of reinvestment emerges not merely as a financial principle but as the lifeline that ensures sustained growth, relevance and prosperity. This chapter delves into the critical role of reinvesting in your business, emphasising that depreciation is not a tax-centric line item but the minimum investment required to stay ahead in the competitive landscape. By continuously improving and evolving your business, not only do you capture the attention of customers and staff, but you also ensure that your enterprise does not merely survive but thrives in the long run.

```
Depreciation – Beyond Taxation,
a Strategic Necessity
```

Understanding depreciation not just as a tax-saving line in your P&L but as the baseline investment needed to keep your business competitive is paramount. The assets that depreciate over time are often the very lifeblood of your operations. Regularly reinvesting in these assets ensures that your business infrastructure remains robust, efficient and capable of meeting evolving demands.

```
The Continuous Evolution
– Staying Ahead in a
Changing Landscape
```

Business landscapes are dynamic, subject to technological advancements, shifting consumer preferences and market trends. The imperative to reinvest lies in the acknowledgment that standing still in such an environment is synonymous with falling behind. Reinvestment allows your business to evolve continually, adapting to new challenges and staying ahead of the curve.

```
Visible Improvements – Noteworthy
to Customers and Staff
```

Customers are astute observers, and staff members are keenly attuned to the state of the business they work for. Reinvesting in your enterprise is not a clandestine operation; it is a visible commitment to improvement. Whether it's updating facilities, adopting innovative technologies, or enhancing product/service quality, visible improvements resonate with both customers and staff, fostering a sense of pride and loyalty.

Beyond Personal Gain – Your Business is Not Your Personal Bank

The notion of viewing your business solely as a personal bank account is a pitfall that hinders growth. Reinvesting necessitates a shift in perspective – from viewing profits solely as personal gains to recognising them as the lifeblood of your business. This paradigm shift paves the way for strategic decisions that prioritise the long-term health and prosperity of the enterprise.

The Ripple Effect of Reinvestment – Multiplying Returns

Reinvestment has a compounding effect on your business. The initial investment in technology, staff training, or infrastructure improvements can multiply returns in terms of increased efficiency, customer satisfaction and market relevance. Each reinvestment becomes a catalyst that propels the business forward, creating a ripple effect of positive outcomes.

Strategic Vision – The Foundation for Sustained Success

Reinvestment is not a haphazard endeavour; it requires a strategic vision. Successful entrepreneurs recognise that reinvesting is not merely a financial transaction but a fundamental component of their business strategy. It involves aligning financial resources with long-term goals, anticipating industry trends and making deliberate choices that fortify the foundation of sustained success.

The Evergreen Legacy of Reinvestment

In the narrative of business success, reinvestment is not a one-time act but an ongoing commitment to growth and evolution. By understanding that depreciation is not merely a tax line item but a strategic necessity, entrepreneurs can propel their businesses to new heights. Reinvestment is not just a financial transaction; it is the legacy of a business that refuses to stand still, continually reaching for excellence and ensuring a future that is not merely prosperous but evergreen.

CHAPTER 43

The Bohemian Bali Dream
A New Venture, a Fresh Canvas

After the ebb and flow of business partnerships, corporate entanglements and the transformative renewal of Byron Fresh, the time had come for a solo venture. This was to be a venture unencumbered by partners, corporate oversight, or compromises – a canvas for the unrestrained pursuit of dreams and passions.

Revisiting Unfulfilled Dreams

The vision was not entirely new; it was a revisiting of old plans that hadn't unfolded as desired in the past. This time, the commitment was unwavering, the direction clear and the conditions non-negotiable. The venture would be a creative expression, a manifestation of aspirations, devoid of financial compulsions.

A Boutique Hotel in Bali

The dream took the shape of a boutique hotel, a small haven of understated luxury, an intimate space where guests would feel not like visitors but cherished guests in a place they never wanted to leave. The inspiration drew from a mosaic of personal travel experiences and a business philosophy cultivated over the years.

The Essence of The Bohemian Bali

'The Bohemian Bali' was more than a hotel; it was a concept. It embodied the spirit of bohemian living – artistic, stylish and unconstrained by conventional architecture or etiquette. The vision aimed to create an environment where individuality thrived, where every corner spoke of the eclectic stories woven into the fabric of the place.

Passion-Driven, Not Profit-Driven

Unlike previous ventures, the driving force behind 'The Bohemian Bali' was not financial gain. Instead, it was fuelled by passion – a desire to craft a space that resonated with the soul, where creativity flowed freely and guests could immerse themselves in a unique, immersive experience.

Choosing Bali

Bali, with its rich cultural tapestry, vibrant atmosphere and a conducive economic environment, emerged as the ideal canvas for this venture. The allure of creating a haven amidst Bali's natural beauty and cultural richness complemented the vision of 'The Bohemian Bali'.

An Artistic Odyssey Begins

Plans were set into motion for the artistic odyssey in Bali. This venture promised to be a culmination of a lifetime of experiences, learnings and the unwavering belief that a business, at its core, could be an artistic expression – a canvas painted with the strokes of passion, individuality and the boundless spirit of the bohemian.

The Bohemian Bali Dream Unfolds

As this chapter unfolds, it marks the beginning of a new adventure – an odyssey to bring 'The Bohemian Bali' to life. With a heart full of dreams and a spirit untethered, the journey into the realms of creativity, hospitality and the bohemian ethos commences.**

CHAPTER 44

Chasing Visions in Canggu
Quest for the Perfect Canvas

Jetting off to Bali marked the beginning of a quest – a quest to find the perfect canvas for 'The Bohemian Bali'. Bali, a land of dreams and contrasts, presented itself as a giant building site, a cacophony of nationalities, ideas and countless half-finished projects. Amidst this vibrant chaos, finding a gap in the market seemed daunting, yet the allure of Bali's energy and potential beckoned.

Staying Grounded in Ubud, Soaking in Seminyak and Surfing in Canggu

The exploration journey took us through the heart of Bali – Ubud, with its spiritual resonance; Seminyak, pulsating with cosmopolitan vibes; and Canggu, a coastal haven brimming with surfers and creative souls. Each place infused us with its unique spirit, but it was in Canggu that we felt the familiar resonance of the Byron vibe – youthful energy, vibrant dining scenes and a creative hub in the making.

Navigating the Sea of Dreams

In a sea of dreams and construction, the challenge was not just finding land but finding the right energy. Bali, a melting pot of aspirations, offered encounters with numerous agents and acquaintances, each with a different story. The market was competitive, and many dreams lay shattered amidst the ongoing building frenzy.

Trusting Instincts and Meeting Laurent

Amidst the challenges, a chance encounter with Laurent, a French national and builder living in Bali, proved serendipitous. Beyond being an agent, Laurent became a trusted guide and facilitator. His friendly, honest demeanour resonated with our vision, and we found ourselves relying on instincts – a departure from the meticulous corporate processes of the past.

Choosing Canggu as the Bohemian Canvas

Identifying Canggu as the canvas for our dreams, we circled in on a small block of land. The area's similarity to the Byron vibe, with surfers, vibrant cafés and a creative community, captured our hearts. The quest for land evolved into a collaboration with Laurent, who went beyond his role, assisting in all facets – acquiring land, setting up a company, navigating bureaucratic intricacies and even securing investor visas.

A Friend, Guide and More

Laurent wasn't just an agent; he became a friend and guide in this journey. His multifaceted support exemplified the essence of collaboration – a coming together of energies to manifest a shared dream. With Canggu chosen as the backdrop, the stage was set for 'The Bohemian Bali' to unfold – a tapestry woven with passion, creativity and the spirit of bohemia.**

CHAPTER 45

Designing Dreams – The Bohemian Bali Unveiled Conceiving the Concept

With the land secured, the next phase of the journey unfolded – a journey of design, creativity and redefining paradigms. The vision for 'The Bohemian Bali' wasn't just about creating a hotel; it was about crafting an experience. I envisioned a unique, tropical warehouse-style concept – an ode to the unconventional, a haven for the bohemian spirit.

A Canvas of Creativity

Inspiration struck in the form of an old warehouse – a relic with stories to tell. Sketches transformed the vision into tangible blueprints, and the concept of a sensual, artistic and daring haven for couples began to take shape. Stepping away from the conventional whites and beiges of Bali, I sought to infuse the design with darkness, sensuality and a touch of the erotic – a true sanctuary for the like-minded traveller seeking an unconventional lifestyle, even if only for a holiday.

Tailoring for the Bohemian Spirit

The design aimed for a niche market, targeting the bohemian spirit. The concept embraced exclusivity – suites only, crafted for couples who sought a sensual escape. Every detail, from the layout to the colour palette, resonated with the essence of bohemia. The spaces weren't just rooms; they were canvases waiting to be filled with stories, passion and the eclectic energy of the bohemian lifestyle.

Music, Art and Individuality

Music became a cornerstone of the design, weaving its magic through the spaces. Local artists were to be integral contributors, infusing the suites with their unique expressions. Each suite was envisioned as an individual masterpiece, a fusion of art, sensuality and the distinctive energy that defines the bohemian soul.

Anticipating Antiques

Before the first brick was laid, the project came to life through the acquisition of antique pieces, eclectic art and captivating chandeliers. These treasures were more than decor – they were integral to the narrative, waiting to find their place in the suites and contribute to the ambiance of The Bohemian Bali.

The Birth of a Name

In the early stages, before the concept had fully materialised, the name declared itself. 'Bohemian' encapsulated the essence of the project – an ode to free spirits, unconventional journeys and a celebration of the art of living. The name became a beacon guiding the creation of this unique retreat.

Years of Ambitions Unleashed

The design process wasn't just a task; it was an embodiment of years of creative ambitions. Every stroke of the pen, every choice of colour and every piece of art reflected a commitment to crafting a space where the bohemian spirit could find solace, expression and a home away from home.

The Bohemian Bali – A Tapestry Unfolding:

As the sketches evolved into plans and the plans into reality, Bohemian Bali started to transcend the realm of dreams. It was becoming a tapestry – a tapestry woven with passion, creativity and the spirit of bohemia, poised to offer an experience unlike any other in the heart of Bali.**

CHAPTER 46

Pandemic Pause – Re-evaluating Ambitions A Global Standstill

As the world grappled with the unforeseen disruption of the COVID-19 pandemic, our plans for The Bohemian Bali were momentarily suspended. Travel restrictions and lockdowns confined us to our homes, providing an unexpected pause in the relentless pursuit of our dreams.

A Trusted Ally in Uncertain Times

In the midst of uncertainty, Laurent emerged as a steadfast ally. Entrusted with representing our interests in Bali, his guidance and support proved invaluable. Our instinct to choose him as a partner aligned with our values, and as travel became a distant luxury, his local presence became our bridge to the unfolding situation in Bali.

Adapting to the New Normal

The pandemic reshaped our daily lives, but it also provided a unique opportunity for reflection. Stationed on our property in the Byron hinterland, we found solace in the tranquillity of the Australian hinterland. Unexpectedly, government support became a crucial lifeline, allowing us to weather the storm and re-evaluate our priorities.

Navigating Challenges in Byron

While the pandemic brought moments of introspection, it also accentuated the challenges faced in the Byron business partnership. The turbulent times underscored the need for change, prompting a decision to exit the partnership that had run its course.

An Unexpected Offer

As the pandemic's grip began to loosen, a surprising turn of events unfolded – an unsolicited offer emerged to purchase the Byron business. Seizing the opportunity, negotiations ensued, and the sale was eventually completed. The timing, seemingly orchestrated by fate, aligned perfectly with our need for a fresh start.

Free from Past Constraints

The sale marked the end of a chapter, liberating us from business partnerships that had outlived their usefulness. Byron was no longer a tether; it had become a memory. The windfall from the sale offered financial freedom, unlocking resources essential for our ambitions with The Bohemian.

Resuming the Journey

With the shackles of partnerships cast aside, I found myself free to resume the journey towards The Bohemian Bali. This pause, forced upon me by a global crisis, had not hindered our dreams – it had refined them. The values and experiences accumulated over a diverse business journey were now poised to shape a venture built on authenticity and a commitment to crafting an unparalleled experience.**

CHAPTER 47

**The Bohemian Bali – A
Dream Realised Unveilling
the Bohemian Bali**

As the restrictions lifted, travel became more than a longing – it became a reality. The completion of The Bohemian Bali marked the fruition of a dream, an endeavour unmarred by compromise. Stepping onto the grounds of our boutique hotel, the feeling was surreal, almost too good to be true.

**A Harmonious Fusion of
Dreams and Reality**

The success of The Bohemian Bali exceeded expectations. The distinctive design, inspired by a tropical warehouse aesthetic, resonated with the Bohemian spirit we sought to capture. Suites infused with sensuality and artistry welcomed couples seeking a unique escape. The ambiance, a departure from the typical Balinese palette, found its own rhythm, creating a harmonious fusion of dreams turned into reality.

Building a Team in Bali

Embarking on this venture meant immersing ourselves in a new culture – working alongside the Balinese. Building a team in Bali proved to be a pleasure. The Balinese ethos of warmth and hospitality seamlessly blended with our commitment to authenticity. The result was a team that not only understood the vision but also contributed to the positive energy that permeated the bohemian.

Instant Success and Financial Harmony

The Bohemian Bali wasn't just a business; it was a manifestation of passion. The positive energy and genuine commitment to providing an unparalleled experience translated into instant success. Financial harmony, a stark contrast to previous ventures, became a testament to the belief that a business rooted in authenticity could thrive.

Guests Feel the Difference

Guest reviews have echoed the sentiment – the realisation of what we set out to achieve. The heart and soul infused into The Bohemian were palpable. The guests felt the difference – a retreat that went beyond the ordinary, a haven crafted with intention and care.

The Bohemian's Story Unfolding

The completion of The Bohemian Bali wasn't the end; it was the beginning of a new chapter. More dreams were waiting to come alive, more ventures to explore and a business with a soul that was only beginning its story.

The Bohemian's Legacy

As the legacy of the Bohemian continued to unfold, its impact extended beyond the confines of a boutique hotel. It became a testament to the power of dreams undeterred, a reminder that businesses rooted in passion and authenticity could redefine success.*

CHAPTER 48

Weaving of Experience

As I reflect on my journey, woven with threads of diverse experiences, the overarching theme reveals itself – a tale of leadership, people, instinct, positive energy and the infusion of passion into the heart of business. Each chapter unfolds as a lesson, a building stone for the next and a testament to the transformative power of a life dedicated to growth and fulfilment.

Leadership: The Beacon of Influence

From the early days at Sport Scheck Munich to navigating the complexities of Starbucks corporate dynamics, the impact of leadership stands as a beacon throughout my journey.

Good leadership fosters trust, loyalty and a positive team culture. Bad leadership, as witnessed in various chapters, stifles creativity and sows seeds of discontent. The ability to inspire, adapt and lead with integrity emerges as a cornerstone lesson.

Impact on People: The Heartbeat of Business

The heartbeat of every business is its people. From the team at Maroubra McDonald's to the collaborative efforts in opening Starbucks Australia, the essence of success lies in fostering connections, trust and loyalty. People are not just employees; they are the soul of a business. Positive relationships create positive environments, and a business's success is intricately tied to the well-being of its people.

Instinctive Actions: The Navigator Within

Throughout my journey, instinct emerged as a guiding force. The decision to explore Starbucks in Canada, the intuitive exit from McDonald's, and the move to Byron Bay – all were guided by a deep-seated intuition. Instinctive actions, when aligned with experience, proved to be a reliable navigator, steering towards purposeful ventures and away from potential pitfalls.

Positive Energy: Fuel for Success

Positive energy is the lifeblood that fuels success. From the vibrant team culture at Maroubra McDonald's to the rejuvenation of the Byron business, the impact of positive energy is unmistakable. A positive work environment not only enhances productivity but also shapes the essence of the business, creating a resonance that extends to customers and beyond.

Passion: The Driving Force

Passion, the driving force behind ventures like The Bohemian Bali, is a magnetic energy that transcends financial metrics. From the early days at Hotel Hofer Alm to the bold move with Starbucks, passion-infused purpose into every endeavour. It is the unwavering commitment to creating something meaningful that transforms businesses from mere profit centres to soulful entities.

Financial Results: The Scorecard, Not the Maestro

While financial results serve as a scorecard, they should not dictate the symphony of management. The journey from McDonald's to Starbucks and beyond reiterated that financial success is a natural outcome of purposeful actions, positive energy and a passion-infused approach. Let financial results be the measurement of success, not the force driving decisions.

Lessons as Building Stones

Every chapter, from the early lessons at Sport Scheck Munich to the completion of The Bohemian Bali, contributes building stones to an evolving narrative. The unwritten chapters beckon with the promise of more growth, more challenges and more fulfilment. As I stand at this juncture, I recognise that each experience, whether triumphant or challenging, has shaped me – not just as a businessperson but as an individual on a continuous journey of learning and growth.

Woven with the threads of leadership, positive energy, passion and instinct, tells a story of resilience, adaptability and the pursuit of a life less ordinary. As I turn the pages of my own narrative, I embrace the unwritten chapters with enthusiasm, knowing that the lessons learned and the values upheld will continue to guide the way. It's not just a business journey; it's a journey of self-discovery, relationships and the pursuit of a purposeful and fulfilling life.

Postscript: Unfolding Realities – Why These Final Chapters Were Written

When *Dreamweaver: The Odyssey of an Entrepreneur* was first published, I believed the story had come full circle. It was a natural pause in a long and deeply personal journey—a moment to reflect, to take stock, and perhaps to let go. But life, as it tends to do, had other plans.

This second edition includes two new chapters that were not part of the original manuscript. They weren't written retrospectively but emerged organically as events unfolded—unexpected turns in a journey that continues to evolve. I felt compelled to include them not for the sake of completeness, but because they speak to where I am now and to where the world, particularly the one I operate in, seems to be heading.

The first of these chapters is a continuation of the journey. It shares what came next after the original story was told—the challenges I didn't see coming, the moments of doubt, the quiet victories, and the questions that remain unresolved. It's less a conclusion and more a new beginning, a reminder that entrepreneurial paths are rarely straight and never truly finished.

The second chapter addresses a topic I can no longer ignore: overtourism. As someone who has built a hospitality business in one of the world's most visited destinations, I've become increasingly aware of the tension between creating meaningful guest experiences and preserving the very places that draw those guests in the first place. This chapter is not written from a distance, but from within the reality of what it means to be part of the problem, and hopefully, part of a better way forward.

I chose to publish this second edition because the story had more to say. These new chapters don't alter what came before—they deepen it. They acknowledge that no dream exists in isolation, and that every act of creation is part of a larger, ever-shifting landscape.

CHAPTER 49

Afterthought – Bali and Becoming

Bali, ever so mystical and layered, has a way of revealing itself over time—not just in what you see, but in what you feel.

After the whirlwind of the pandemic, something unexpected and beautiful emerged. The island, stripped of its usual chaos and congestion, softened into something more intimate. No roaring scooters, no waves of tour buses—just quiet temples, open roads, and a renewed humility among locals and expats alike. In a strange way, it felt like Bali was breathing again, and with it, we too had a chance to exhale.

The Bohemian, our beloved project, blossomed in this new rhythm. With fewer distractions and more attention to detail, we honed what we had built. The guests came, slowly at first, then steadily. The reviews flowed in, glowing and generous. Our occupancy was strong, and there was a palpable sense that something special had taken root. It was no longer just a boutique hotel; it was an experience people remembered. A story they carried home with them.

And then, the long-standing dream circled back—Design Hotels.

For years, whenever I traveled, I sought out Design Hotels. They weren't just places to stay. They were places to be. Stories told through texture and light, conversations held through architecture, and an unspoken code among their owners: passion before profit, creativity over conformity.

So when discussions began with their Berlin office, it felt like coming full circle. The emails turned into calls. Calls turned into negotiations. And then came the call—the one I believed would finalize our membership.

It started warmly, as expected. Then came the pause. The soft, but unmistakable pivot.

Alba, my liaison at Design Hotels, gently broke the news: while they adored the concept and appreciated the design, The Bohemian lacked two vital components for full membership—communal space and a true F&B experience.

It was a moment of disappointment, no doubt. But more than that, it was a challenge. A spark.

I had always believed The Bohemian would evolve in layers, and this was simply the next one. I told Alba, without hesitation, that I was already planning to address these exact elements. That wasn't entirely true at the time—but it soon became so.

We began sketching ideas for an expansion: a shared pool with sun loungers, a small one-table eatery, additional rooms, storage, and staff space. The timing aligned with the opportunity to acquire more land next door, and somehow, as it so often happens in Bali, things began to fall into place.

Designing this next phase was trickier. The space was tighter, and I didn't want to just replicate what we had. I wanted to evolve— maintaining the soul of the original but pushing the aesthetic forward. Still bohemian, but with a more contemporary edge.

With Fransisca, our brilliant interior designer, we went to work. Sketches became plans, and plans became reality. Slowly. Painfully slowly at times. Building in Bali is not for the faint-hearted. There's willingness, yes. But skill and consistency? Often elusive. The bathroom tiles alone were redone four times before they passed muster.

And yet, the frustrations were tempered by the kindness and grace of the people around me. There's a certain patience that the Balinese carry that makes even the most maddening delays somehow tolerable. I found myself not just managing a build—but growing with it.

The Bohemian team rose to the occasion. They were the quiet heroes of this phase—balancing the chaos of construction with the serenity we promised every guest. The hotel stayed open. The guests stayed happy. And I stayed on site, living and breathing the project, day and night.

That period of being embedded with the team, of sourcing art together, moving furniture, solving problems shoulder-to-shoulder—it changed the dynamics. We were no longer just employer and staff. We were a unit. There was trust. Respect. Shared stories.

Around us, construction boomed—neighbours to the left, right, and behind all started building too. The Bohemian was suddenly an island in a sea of scaffolding. But even that didn't stop us. It may have even made us stronger.

But none of this—none of it—would have come together without the unwavering support of Kamon. My biggest supporter. My life partner. The one who, with gentle strength, carried me through moments of doubt. Countless phone calls filled with encouragement, laughter, and sometimes just the quiet reassurance that I wasn't alone. Kamon visited often, and those visits were more than comforting—they were transformative.

Together we wandered through markets and galleries, sourcing art and decorations. We stood in unfinished rooms debating where to hang what, which fabric to use, which light to soften a space. Each decision, each moment, became a shared act of creation.

Kamon's eye for detail was invaluable. She has a remarkable ability to see the small things that make a space come alive—the little textures, the way light hits a surface, how a color makes a room feel. There is no doubt in my mind that her natural talent for making and creating warm, welcoming environments was critical in shaping the final feel of The Bohemian. She has an intuitive sense of harmony, of balance, of beauty—and that sense is now woven into every corner of the hotel.

A true wingman. To have her on my side throughout this journey was not just helpful—it was everything.

Without this support—not just physical, but deeply emotional and grounding—The Bohemian would never have become what it is now.

After more than a year, the extension was finally complete. And with it, came the long-awaited moment—Design Hotels accepted us.

We were in.

To see our property listed among those I had admired for so many years—those little hotels that dared to be different, to be heartfelt, to be artful—was surreal. Even more so knowing that we were also joining the Marriott Bonvoy network, unlocking a global audience and creating an entirely new rhythm for bookings.

That moment was quiet, but powerful. No grand celebration. Just a deep, private pride.

The Bohemian, born of sketches on scrap paper, evolved through sweat, persistence, love, and partnership, was now part of something bigger. And yet, it never lost its soul.

Now, as I sit with the next phase quietly forming in my mind, I can't help but wonder—what next?

DREAMWEAVER

There's always a whisper of worry that comes with contentment. The fear that maybe this was the peak. That perhaps, you've already lived your best chapter.

But if Bali has taught me anything, it's this: the island doesn't let you stay still. It hums. It shifts. It invites you, again and again, to begin.

And so, I will.

CHAPTER 50

Crossroads – The Price of Paradise

It's hard to say exactly when the shift happened. Maybe it crept in slowly, disguised behind sunsets and smoothie bowls, or maybe it came like a wave—loud, fast, and impossible to ignore. But somewhere along the way, travel changed.

Bali changed.

But this isn't just about Bali. It's about everywhere. It's about what travel used to be—and what it seems to be becoming.

There was a time when travel was about crossing borders in the hope of widening your own. It was about culture, not clout. About connection, not content. You went somewhere not to say you'd been there, but to be there. To listen. To taste. To understand. You learned how other people lived, not to compare, but to appreciate. It wasn't always comfortable—but that was the point.

Now, I watch with concern as that spirit fades. Replaced, often, by something much more curated and far less curious.

It's a phenomenon best described as Instagram Tourism—a kind of frantic chase for the next perfect shot, often at the expense of the very place being visited. It's no longer about Bali's temples or its ceremonies. It's about you in front of them. And it's not just here. From Iceland to Istanbul, Paris to Patagonia—it's the same poses, same captions, same cafés, and same filtered storylines. The unique is becoming uniform.

And while I understand the desire to share beauty—and yes, I too have taken my fair share of photos—what I'm talking about goes beyond that. It's a mindset. An approach. An extraction.

Because when we visit without truly seeing, consume without contributing, and build without boundaries, we turn sacred places into backdrops. Cultures into commodities.

Bali, in many ways, has become the poster child for this evolution. Or perhaps, revolution.

In 2023, Bali welcomed 5.2 million international arrivals, a stunning return after the stillness of COVID-19. Just ten years ago, in 2013, that number stood at around 3.3 million. The growth is relentless, unregulated, and increasingly unsustainable. The roads are gridlocked, often for hours just to reach the airport. The rice fields are vanishing beneath cement and steel. Construction booms with no limit, no pause, no regard.

It's not just tourists taking from the island—many locals too are cashing in. Who can blame them? When opportunity knocks, it's hard to say no. But at what cost?

Entire villages are being bulldozed for beach clubs and boutique developments. Sacred spaces are being invaded for that one perfect photo. Waste and plastic pile up in rivers, beaches erode under the weight of "progress," and the spiritual heartbeat of Bali—its customs, its ceremonies, its way of life—is fading into the background.

And here's the strange, bitter irony: tourists come seeking "authenticity" while unknowingly destroying the very thing they came for.

Even the act of traveling—once romantic and adventurous—has become a kind of choreographed ordeal. Herded through endless security lines, subjected to random searches, crammed into budget airlines and then spilled out into shopping districts filled with fake Louis Vuitton bags, western menus, and industrial-strength air conditioning. Is this still travel? Or just mass consumerism in a prettier costume?

The late Naomi Klein wrote in her book *No Logo* about the way brands colonize space, ideas, and eventually culture. That's exactly where we are now. Travel itself has been branded. Adventure has been corporatized. Experience has become performance.

Bali—this place I love, where I've chosen to live, build, and create—is teetering on the edge. And what's happening here is a warning, a glimpse into what global tourism may become if left unchecked.

And yet, I believe in another path.

We can still choose to support what's real. To seek out the small. The slow. The soulful. We can stay in traditional, boutique accommodations—places built with heart, not just profit. We can avoid the traps and take the less-traveled road. We can learn, not just consume.

We can ask: Who built this place? Whose story am I stepping into? What can I leave behind that isn't waste?

This reflection doesn't come without contradiction. I see it—I am it. Tourism has been the thread through my life: from Austria to Australia to Bali. It's what I've worked in, built with, and lived by. So yes, call me a hypocrite if you must. I accept the criticism on the cheek.

But my hope is that we can evolve. That we can become not just tourists, but travelers again. That we can hold space for places—truly hold space for them, not just occupy them.

At The Bohemian, we try. Every day. We try to offer something deeper, something grounded in craft, culture, and connection. But the truth is—it only works if our guests meet us there. If they're willing to do the same.

Because Bali—and the world—doesn't need more selfies.

It needs more soul.

EPILOGUE

As we reach the conclusion of this journey through the pages of personal experiences, insights and lessons in entrepreneurship, it's imperative to acknowledge that what transpired within these chapters is not gospel. The diverse narratives, strategies and perspectives shared are a testament to the multifaceted nature of the entrepreneurial voyage.

In the journey of my own experiences and learnings, I've encountered varied approaches to business, each shaped by the unique paths of individuals I've had the privilege to observe and learn from. Success, a term often sought after and measured in countless ways, is as personal as the journey itself. The place I stand today, marked by what I deem as success, may not align with the aspirations or definitions of others, and that's perfectly valid.

The heart of this entrepreneurial odyssey lies in the understanding that success is a nuanced concept, being subjective and deeply personal. What worked for me may not be a universal blueprint. Yet, within the diversity of strategies and outcomes, there lies a common thread – the unquenchable thirst for learning.

The more I traversed the intricate landscapes of business, the more apparent it became that knowledge is an ever-expanding horizon. No summit exists where one can proclaim to know everything. In fact, the paradox reveals itself: the more one learns, the more one realises the vast expanse of the unknown.

Life, a relentless teacher, whispers lessons in every challenge, success, failure and unexpected turn. The key lies not in claiming mastery but in remaining a perpetual student, receptive to the ever-changing melodies of the entrepreneurial symphony.

So, as we close this chapter of shared experiences, let it serve as a reminder that the journey is ongoing, and there is always more to discover, explore and comprehend. The pursuit of knowledge and the willingness to listen to the subtle cues of life are the compasses that guide us through the uncharted territories of entrepreneurship.

May your own journey be marked by continuous learning, adaptability and a steadfast commitment to listen and evolve. The entrepreneurial odyssey is a story still unfolding, with the potential for endless chapters that transcend the limitations of what we think we know.

As the final pages turn, let them echo with the resounding truth that the pursuit of knowledge is a lifelong adventure and the true measure of success lies not just in the destination but in the ever-enriching voyage itself.

www.ingramcontent.com/pod-product-compliance
Lightning Source LLC
Chambersburg PA
CBHW040107100526
44584CB00029BA/3863